SOUL SKETCHES

2nd Edition

TIM RITTER

Soul Sketches – Second Edition - Copyright © 2020 – Tim Ritter
All cover art copyright © 2020
All Rights Reserved

No part of this book may be reproduced or transmitted in any form or by any means, electronic or mechanical, including photocopying, recording, or by any information storage and retrieval system, except in the case of brief quotations embodied in critical reviews and certain other noncommercial uses permitted by copyright law, without permission in writing from the author.

The basic happenings are true: real events, actual locations and names represent real people. The events and conversations in the book have been set down to the best of the author's ability.

Cover Design – Corey Ritter

Publishing Coordinator – Sharon Kizziah-Holmes

Paperback-Press
an imprint of A & S Publishing
A & S Holmes, Inc.

ISBN -13: 978-1-951772-04-8

DEDICATION

This book is dedicated to my wife Lisa, in eternal gratitude for her wanting me to "just be Tim"

CONTENTS

Dedication	iii
Introduction	1
The Poet and the Woman	4
Tongue-Tied	6
First Date	10
An Unfinished Romance	12
Talking to You	14
A Certain Silence	15
Two Lovers	16
You Are My Star	17
Without You	19
Facing the Bully	20
A Few Thoughts Before I Resign	26
Life by Numbers	27
Dammit Mom	28
Control	29
A Formal Apology	30
Call Me	31
Driving…Thinking…	32
That Boy	33
Coming Full Circle, On a Roller Coaster	35
A Few Parting Thoughts	43
Grandpa	45
Requiem	47
Ode to Aunt Doty	48
I Quit	51
Never Fear	52
Reflections	54
A Note to Si	56
The Bridge	58
A One-sided Chat with the Dragon	62
Twitch	63
Losing It	65
Memorial Night	66
The Terror Inside	70
The Mirror	71
Purgatory	72
Gone	73
Elevator Girl	74
Breakdown	79
I Lost	81
Breaking the Horse	83
Making Love to the Wolf	85
The Door	86

Thoughts of Bleeding	88
Waving Each Other Goodnight	89
Connie	91
Alone on Valentine's Day (Again)	94
Coffee at Denny's – A Collection	95
Hardening the Heart	99
It Ends Now	100
Headphones	101
Night Love	102
The Game	103
If I Could Feel Your Love	105
Candelabras and Scarlet Tights	106
Christmas Past and Present	112
Joseph's Prayer	113
Chicago Fog	114
Kidney Stone #3	115
Love and Candy	117
Soul Mate	119
The Beach	121
Success	122
The Eleventh Hour	123
Stage Blood and French Fries	126
A Soldier's Tale	130
The Shoebox Hat Story	133
A Long Farewell	135
Tummy Trouble Blues	136
My Boot Passion	137
Don't Forget to Breathe	138
Amidst the Squirm	140
Lay Down	142
Wearing the Boots	143
Passion	145
The Ride	146
A Dance with Jami	147
Missing You	150
Sunday Morning	151
Devotion	152
My Love, Asleep	153
Proclaiming My Love	154
The Heavens	155
Thoughts of Someone	156
More…	157
Valentine's Day 2018	158
About the Author	160

Introduction

My journey into writing began in elementary school, attempting to write little ditties about my pets at home. The ditties all turned out to sound pretty much the same, with classic meaningful lines like "My cat Sam, he really is a ham." I continued to write whenever possible, and spent the next few years of my childhood quietly hoping to say something more important, searching for my voice.

Then in junior high school, with hormones raging, I had a crush on a girl. Actually I had a crush on most of the girls. This one in particular ended up becoming my girlfriend for a whole week or two. Ever the hopeless romantic, I somehow gathered up the gumption to write three poems for her.

Fast forward to college: I found myself going through some interesting experiences, and wanted to keep record of the things going on around me, the thoughts in my head and the feelings in my heart. I kept a journal in a simple spiral notebook, but grew bored with the mundane narrative style that I found myself writing on the pages, filling the lines with what happened that day, etc. My freshman year I took an English class with Dr. Eugene Warren, professor and poet. The class offered the opportunity to play with normal writing styles and alternatives to standard grammar. I started applying those creative ideas to my writing and liked what I came up with. Thus the collection that became Soul Sketches began.

The first release of ***Soul Sketches*** in 2012 was a collection of poems only, which I wrote between 1985 and 2011. Throughout those years several friends, upon reading the collection in its handwritten form, told me I should publish it and share my thoughts. So I did and was quite pleased with the response.

Within a few years, though, I looked at the collection and wondered if I could do something more with it. I felt like several poems within the book should have perhaps been left out, or at least reworked. I also discovered I wasn't happy with the original *Untitled Works* section, and that I should come up with titles for the poems which I previously felt I could not name. Additionally, I wanted to add some short stories, and even perhaps introductions to some of the poems, to help people understand the inspiration or point behind my writing.

So, in 2019, seven years after the initial release, I revisited ***Soul Sketches*** and turned it into something beyond my original vision. I added new poems as well, which I wrote in celebration of finding love again.

So, you now hold in your hands ***Soul Sketches, 2nd Edition***, with which I am quite pleased, and hope you will be too.

As I said in the introduction to the original book, one of the main driving points behind these writings is "Have you ever felt this way?" It remains my sincere hope that you find a little bit of yourself within these pages, and that you are also entertained. Feel free to laugh, cry, or get angry, in celebration that you are alive and a feeling, loving human being.

Thank you for reading.

The Poet and the Woman

"Every woman should have a poet," she said.
But the truth is,
Every poet
Should have a woman
Like her.

Odes of Love
Can flow freely from the pen
(Surprisingly) in times
Of extreme loneliness
Or when love exists within
Unshared,
Unappreciated,
Unreturned.

Such Odes
Are filled
With hopeful supposition
And dreams
Of what could be.

But to the Poet
Who has the Love
Of which he has always dreamt,
The words of Love,
Shared,
Appreciated,
Returned;

The Words,
Take on new meaning
And bring a joyful, loving tear to his eye
As he speaks them.

The Words of Love
Have returned
And the Heart again beats
With great joy.

Thank you,
For bring the Woman
For the Poet.

Tongue-Tied

I could have said anything at that moment. But that's what came out?!

In late 2016, Lisa and I discovered we were interested in each other. We were already friends, and had been for a couple of years. Secretly I thought she was beautiful, more than once saying to myself "Why can't I have someone like her?" in the midst of my fifty-something single life. But I never expected her to return the interest.

But there it was. Newly single, she contacted me one night and made it clear she was interested. We had a wonderful time getting to know each other on a much deeper level as we exchanged messages back and forth. Initially arranging a date was nearly impossible due to our busy lives and conflicting schedules.

Finally, after nearly two months of texting, we decided it was time for a date, some serious face-to-face time. Enough with virtual communication; we needed to visit in person to see if this thing between us was worth pursuing.

Our schedules came together one Monday afternoon. That day I had already requested the afternoon off due to my furnace crapping out at home. She too was available then, so we made plans for a date at a lunch spot near my work.

That morning I could hardly contain my excitement. I normally left for lunch at 11:30, and counted the minutes leading up to time to shut down my laptop and call it a day. Fortunately no one got in the way as I bounded out the door and took off in my truck for our date.

Pulling into the parking lot of the sandwich shop, I suddenly became aware that I didn't know what type of car she drove. I looked around and didn't see an occupied vehicle, so I assumed she was either already inside and waiting for me, or she hadn't shown up yet. The day was unusually hot, so I chose to wait inside rather than stand outside and work up a sweat. Perspiration is not known to impress on a first date. So inside I went, looking around to see if she was there. No Lisa.

Little did I know that Lisa was two cars away from where I parked, hidden in her little sports car by the large truck parked in the space next to mine. Since I didn't walk around the truck, I never saw her sitting there waiting for me. She saw me, though, as I walked across the lot and into the restaurant. Fumbling nervously with her controls, she later admitted she couldn't get the window down quickly enough to yell at me before I was inside.

After looking around the restaurant and realizing she was not already there, I turned and glanced out the glass door. There, walking toward me, was Lisa. She still had her sunglasses on, and her beautiful red hair and blue and white dress danced about in the breeze. She reached up to run her fingers through her hair. I couldn't breathe; she looked absolutely beautiful.

Then I looked down and saw she was wearing black leather boots. Suddenly it hit me. She had been paying attention. She knew I had a thing for women wearing boots. I had previously written about it on my blog. I realized she must have read it. And to top it all off, the day's weather was not conducive to wearing boots. The area was experiencing a spell of unusually warm weather, so no one else was wearing boots. Except her. She'd worn them just for me.

So as she walked toward the door, hair and dress moving softly in the wind, the heels of her boots making their lovely sound on the pavement, my brain raced, searching for the right thing to say. Gears in my head began to spin and bearing temperatures began to soar. Messages fired back and forth across synapses, ideas for what to say flew through my brain, impulses were sent to my tongue to speak, and urgent signals pleaded for my lungs to start working again and for me to quit holding my breath!

She got to the door as I pushed from inside to open it for

her. She took off her sunglasses and smiled, as I smiled back, leaning in for a quick hug to welcome her.

My mouth begged for a great opening statement:
She looks beautiful.
The gears in my head locked up.
She's wearing boots, dude.
Bearings overheated.
Her eyes are amazing.
Synapses died.
That's a very pretty dress.
Impulses quit arriving at my tongue.
She's been paying attention and decided to wear boots for you, dude.
One quick message was received by my mouth and came out:
As we embraced, I whispered in her ear:
"You little stinker!"

That's what came out… on our first date.

Not "You look beautiful." Not "That's a pretty dress." Not "It's so nice to see you."
Instead, I actually said, "You little stinker."
Fortunately, she did not immediately push me away and leave.

We ordered our food and settled into a small table against a wall, swimming in each other's eyes. We talked, laughed, and even giggled a little. Actually, we giggled more than just a little.

At one point, she got up to excuse herself to the ladies room. After she passed by me, I could not resist the temptation to turn around and watch her. I sat there and studied how her hair cascaded over her shoulders. I noticed how her pretty dress swayed as she walked. And of course I looked at her boots. Smitten, I began to turn back around in my chair, but as I did, I made eye contact with an older lady seated with a friend behind us. She gave me a knowing smile, like she had been watching us all along and figured out we were there on a date. I grinned and turned around in my chair.

Lisa and I enjoyed the rest of that magical first date, and I'm not sure if I drove home afterwards or just floated there. I couldn't wipe the smile from my face. But as soon as I got home, I stood in the bathroom and looked in the mirror in horror:

"Really? All you could say was 'you little stinker?'"

Clearly, I was never going to win Smooth Talker of the Year. Although I'm happy to report that nine months later when I asked her to marry me, the words came out right... finally.

And she said yes.

First Date

Many cycles of the moon
Have passed silently overhead
In the time that I have known you
As a friend.

We have discussed life,
Laughed at our failings,
And walked through ivied halls
As friends.

Your perfume has filled my wanting senses,
Your delicate, curvy form has caught my notice,
And I've wondered many splendored things
While we've been friends.

Till one day…

The day I saw you walking toward me
For that first lunch together
As two adults expressing interest
In one another.

Your pretty dress dancing in the wind
(A bit more than you preferred)
Your boots making their distinctive sound
As you walked, wearing them just for me.

You slipped off your sunglasses
And finally I saw your eyes,
Your beautiful eyes,
And looked deeply
As only nearness can allow…
And I caught my breath…

I lost my ability to speak
(Speak intelligently, anyway)
And three words somehow came out
But I know not from where
As I felt I could say nothing;
At least nothing of any consequence…

Oh, to wrap my arms around you,
Turn you around as we stood among others
And kiss you softly
Did I so desire.

My life changed forever
During those first few moments
And I knew then

That this friend
Was now also
My love.

An Unfinished Romance

The lights are low, the room is full,
As the music begins to play.
I scan the room and catch your eyes
Looking at me in an interesting way.

I smile at you, you smile back,
And I find myself hoping for romance.
But first things first, and so I proceed
To come over and ask you to dance.

We start to dance, the tune is quick
And we're moving along with the crowd
And I have to yell anything I want to say
Because the music is so damn loud!

I ask your name, which is pretty important,
And you tell me with a grin.
Then you ask for mine and I reply,
And you say, "It's nice to meet you, Jim."

"No, Tim!" I correct. I often must.
Those things happen, I suppose,
But now that we've got all that straightened out,
The song is coming to a close!

That song stops, a slow one starts,
And I ask another dance with you.
You answer yes, and the next thing, I guess,
Is for me to wrap my arms around you.

That feeling right there to none can compare,
Holding someone for the first time.
I gently pull you in closer, and you follow suit,
And I begin to fear thoughts in my mind.

I look at you, you are looking at me
And I know what we want to do.
Our lips meet in a warm, soft kiss--
And I rather enjoy it, too.

We smile at each other, and I hold you close
As we dance through the rest of the song.
I find myself seriously wondering
What it would be like to hold you all night long...

TALKING TO YOU

Standing face to face,
So close I could feel you breathing…
Looking into your eyes,
Not knowing whether to let out a giggle
Or just smile.

It would have taken only one more step
To bring you closer in to me
And yet I cannot help but feel
That as I moved
You would have moved too.

As we sat and talked
And smiled and laughed,
Could you feel me shaking,
Quivering,
Trembling?

It was a longing to hold you.
It was a longing to love you.
It was a longing for all of you.

You were close enough to touch.

I wish I would have…

A CERTAIN SILENCE

There is a certain silence of the morning yellow,
At the time just before my alarm sounds.
It's a warm greeting to the new day ahead
And awake I lie looking around.

There is a certain silence of the afternoon gray,
Ere the ominous rumbles of the coming storm.
With wind strongly blowing across an awaiting land
As I sit holding you, soft and warm.

There is a certain silence of the early evening blue,
As we stroll along a narrow sandy beach.
Your hand cupped in mine as the sun's last bit of red
Sinks close to us, barely out of reach.

There is a certain silence of the late night black
At the instant before our lips meet in a kiss...

One January morning in the 1990s, I found myself sitting in a Chicago coffee shop with several of my colleagues from work. Conversations swirled around me, but I busied myself by observing the countless people going about their morning. At one point I spied a young couple enjoying an intimate conversation. So totally wrapped up in each other, they seemed oblivious to the throngs of noisy people around them in the crowded shop, as well as the busy street just outside. I watched their joy and playfulness for quite some time, then began to write…

Two Lovers

Steal a kiss
In the crowded room.

Hold hands under the table.

Whisper your love
In a soft, wet breath.

Two lovers
Dancing
In and out of days
As the city
Roars
Near them

Miles away…

You Are My Star

I stand alone
In the chill of night
And take my place
Beneath the stars

To think of you
And all that you are
In my universe.

I see my own breath
And feel my heart pound
As the silence of night
Deafens.

I reach out to you
As if you were there
To feel your hand
Within mine.

I strain to overcome
The miles between us
And make sense
Of why we must be apart.

I know you're seeing
The same constellations.
We are like those stars—

Mutually attracted,
Miles apart.
Yet we have hope
To close the gap.

And I know we will.
As one tiny little star,
Strongly attracted to another,
Each circling at outrageous speeds,
I have faith.

We'll not just circle forever.
We'll be together soon.

I'll not rest
Until I am in your arms
In this big universe.

WITHOUT YOU

Tell me you can hear me
When I speak your name;
Tell me your feelings will always be the same.

Tell me there's a reason
Why I feel this way;
Tell me why I can't go another day

Without you.

Tell me you can feel me
When I think of you;
Tell me that your heart will always be true.

Tell me you can see me
In your late night dreams;
Life's not half of what it was, it seems

Without you.

Hold me
And tell me
I won't ever have to be

Without you...

FACING THE BULLY

Bullying. What an awful thing, the terrorizing of another human being, whether by torturing their mind or body, just because the bully doesn't like that person for one reason or another. Bullying seems typically associated with teens being victims of such terror, though it knows no age limit. And it's gotten more sophisticated, including utilizing the social media outlets to harass. Horrible.

I must admit, I never was the victim of bullying throughout elementary school. And nothing really substantial ever happened in high school. But when I was 13, in seventh grade, I found myself targeted. It was pure hell. But I never dreamed it would play out the way it did.

To say that I did not adjust well to seventh grade is an understatement. Feeling a bit backward, scared, and unknowingly suffering from severe depression, I did not make a smooth transition from elementary school to junior high. The first quarter I missed at least one day each week, usually feigning some illness or injury that would hopefully keep me at home so that I wouldn't have to deal with that big school, and that big world. It all frightened me terribly.

One day, when I was actually at school and sitting at lunch with my friend Robbie, two rough-looking eighth graders walked by on the other side of the table. Just as they walked in front of me and Robbie, a chair on their side of the table got kicked into Randy, the guy walking in front. Looking back, I know damn good and well that I didn't kick the chair. It had to have been Robbie.

In my mind's terrified eye, I can see it all happening in slow motion. An angry, sinister snarl crept onto Randy's face as he turned toward me. That snarl was directed at me. Instantly sick to my stomach, I wanted to run. To my 13-

year-old timid self, Randy loomed over me, stronger than me, taller than me, meaner than me. I did nothing wrong, but it didn't matter. He thought I kicked the chair into him. Furious, he slammed both hands down onto the table, his frame towering over me like a giant. The snarling lips spoke.

"What the hell is the matter with you, you little pussy?"

"What are you talking about? I didn't do anything!" I pleaded.

"You know exactly what you did! I'm going to beat your ass, boy!"

His buddy Jerry, another leering, snarl-lipped eighth grader with curly dirty-blonde hair, grinned as he watched Randy terrorize me. He leaned down closer to me.

"We are going to kick your ass!" Jerry's maniacal grin scared me even more.

In the meantime my friend Robbie sat there and watched with eyes as big as saucers. I kept telling Randy and Jerry that I didn't know what they were talking about, and that I didn't do anything. They didn't believe me, but eventually left but not before telling me once again that they were going to kick my ass.

Robbie, with eyes still as big as saucers, turned and looked at me as I sat there trembling with fear. He said, "Oh man, what are you going to do?"

I just shrugged and said, "There's nothing I can do."

I wanted to run and never come back to school, but I knew I couldn't do that. And I knew I couldn't tell my parents about it. The last time I had brought up anything pertaining to being mad at a kid at school, Dad told me that if I didn't double up my fist and hit that kid, he was going to double up his fist and hit me. And I was 12. Mom's response to anything like that was even worse. She would always say, "Well you should just tell them you're a lover, not a fighter." I knew saying something that stupid would get me beaten up for sure. So it was useless to talk with anyone at home, because that would just make life more difficult if Dad ever found out. Hmm, that almost makes Dad my own personal bully, doesn't it?

Over the course of the school year, neither Randy nor Jerry ever ended up beating the shit out of me like they threatened. But the threats continued on a weekly basis. When Seventh Grade Hell Week came around, Jerry and Randy were standing in front of us seventh grade boys in the gym before school, pointing out the guys they were going to beat up. When they saw me, they both grinned and said, "We are so going to beat YOU up!"

My friend Billy Vanzandt sat nearby, and when he heard them threaten me, he jumped up and said, "No, no! He's cool, leave him alone!"

For some reason Randy and Jerry listened to him and said, "Nevermind."

Of course, that made me Billy's friend for life.

Eventually Randy took great joy in calling me a name any time he saw me. He would get right up in my face and say "Pussy!" over and over again, then walk away laughing. That went on until the end of the year. I expected to be glad to see the year end, as Randy would move on to high school and leave me alone my eighth-grade year. However, I wasn't out of the woods yet.

Toward the end of seventh grade, my art teacher liked my work and decided that I should go to an art camp at Kansas University in Lawrence that summer, which the school PTA would help fund if my parents paid half the cost. Interestingly enough, Mom and Dad agreed, although they did not lay out any money initially. As details and plans further developed, I learned that an eighth grader was expected to join me for the art camp. I was horrified to learn that it was Randy, the bully. I had no idea he had artistic ability.

I knew I wanted to go to the camp, but was scared to death of what Randy might do to me so many miles from home, especially if we ended up rooming together. I decided to just keep my cool and see what happened. As the end of school neared, I learned that Randy backed out of going to the camp, and the PTA agreed to take what they planned to pay for his attendance and just add it to what they were paying for mine. So that meant my parents didn't have to pay hardly anything to get me enrolled in the camp. And it meant that Randy wouldn't be there to harass me. Whew! So off to the camp I went, and enjoyed it.

Eighth grade went well without Randy in the building. After junior high, I managed to adjust better to high school, and only saw Randy once from a distance when I got there. I didn't know if we were just never in the same hallway or what, but I was glad to be left alone.

Fast forward through life, and about 30 years after that awful seventh grade year, I worked as a plant engineer and maintenance supervisor at a local chemical plant. At one point we hired two new maintenance technicians, and somehow I missed out on the interview process. So on their first day of work, I walked into the office of the other maintenance supervisor, Dennis, to find out their names, so that I could introduce myself. When Dennis told me their names, I nearly fell over. One of them was Randy.

I double-checked the name and asked to see the resume or application he provided. Dennis didn't have either, and asked me what was wrong. I told him if it was the same Randy, he had bullied me in seventh grade.

Dennis looked at me funny and said, "Are you going to be able to work with this guy or are you going to want to beat the shit out of him?"

"I'll be just fine," I said, smiling. But I couldn't help thinking, "I can't wait to see this son-of-a-bitch."

Finally, in walked Randy, and I walked over to him and shook his hand, introducing myself, amazed to see this person in front of me. The bully that made so many threats and said so many awful things to me had, like most of us, put on quite a few pounds since those days, and I couldn't help notice he ended up being a few inches shorter than me. But his personality got me more than anything else. He was docile as a lamb, quiet spoken, and obviously nervous on his first day. The hateful, mean, seemingly angry-at-the-world person no longer appeared to exist.

I didn't say anything further to him that day, nor the next few days, but so many feelings came flooding back, thinking about how he treated me at a vulnerable point in my life, but I knew that time obviously changed this person completely. The entire situation spun around in my head for a while.

One day, after he had been there for a week or so, I was filling in for Dennis, and at some point during the day Randy and I stood in the shop visiting for a moment.

"What's your name again?" he asked.

"Tim Ritter."

"Hmm. Tim Ritter. Tim Ritter. Why do I know that name?"

I knew now was my chance, and I knew how I wanted to play it.

"I'll tell you why," I said, standing up straight, "You and I both went to Study Junior High. You were in eighth grade, I was in seventh."

And that's all I said, and I just stood there and looked at him.

Suddenly I saw the light go on in his eyes. He remembered.

He let out a long, slow, drawn out "Oh yeaaaaaaah," and his face turned red.

"Yep," was all I said, and I walked away.

I wanted to say so many things, but 30 years is a long time to hold onto anything like that, so I let that conversation settle it. I knew who he was, and he knew that I knew who he was, and that I remembered how he treated me.

Randy didn't last long at the chemical plant. He ended up quitting, saying he didn't feel comfortable working around the chemicals onsite. I don't know where he ended up working or what had happened in his life to change him. Looking back, I wish I would have taken the chance to let down the wall and have an honest and open talk with him, to find out what happened, and what made him change so drastically.

Overall, though, it felt good to close a chapter that I hadn't even realized was still open. The bully in him was dead, and the scared little kid in me had long since grown up. That was enough.

A Few Thoughts Before I Resign

You may think yourself wise,
As you have won a couple of battles;
But I will win the war.
Upon me you may have inflicted
A few nicks and cuts;
But you will wear the scars.
For I will emerge the victor
And call it Experience and Knowledge.

~

You say I lack Drive,
Determination,
Dedication.
Yet in you I see a Dumbshit,
A man of Dishonor,
And Divorce in your future.

~

There is honor and dignity
In admitting error.
There is foolishness
In doing nothing about it.

LIFE BY NUMBERS

Please begin with the lighter colors.
They are so cheery and bright.
They cast such a warm glow on all that nears
And reflect so much light.

If you must, bring on the shades next.
Into each Painting these must fall.
Just make them soft, not too harsh.
Make it gradual; I can't at once take them all.

I feel the deep shadows, blacks, blues,
Coming on with great strokes of the Brush.
It is these tones which hurt the worst.
It is these that I fear so much.

So please begin with the light colors.
Give me lots of yellows and whites.
For I know what is coming as the Canvas grows old;
Dark shadows taking over the light.

Dammit Mom

How am I supposed to write this?
It hurts sometimes to remember.
Is healing supposed to hurt like this?

It feels like Grief.

I spent my whole lie trying to please you.

I meant to say "Life".
Typo.

I spent my whole life trying to please you.
I tried to make you happy,
Because I knew it was up to me.

But now that I think about it,
How can a boy bear the burden
Of keeping his mother going?

It wasn't supposed to be that way.
None of it should have happened the way it did.

I should have been allowed to be me.

Dammit Mom.

CONTROL

Lock up your heart,
Keep it hidden for a while.
Wipe that grin off your face,
You've no right to smile.

Goddammit, you fool!
Look at what you've done!
Left yourself wide open again;
Do you see anything you've won?

There is a time and place for everything
And you apparently know neither.
You don't go balls-out from the start;
You didn't think of that, either.

Grow up, already,
You're twenty-two!
If you don't control yourself
What are you going to do?

Control is the key here,
You've got to make it your rule
Or else you're going to wind up again
Looking like a damn fool.

A Formal Apology

We all owe You an apology
For the damage we have done
There's not much left we can do
To reverse what has become.

Your creations are slowly being destroyed
Once gone, never to return.
Precious beings are killed every day
And yearly, countless acres of forests burn.

We've made quite a mockery of You,
Twisting words to satisfy our needs.
Those who claim to be closest to You
Are more concerned with themselves, their greed.

I don't see how You could forgive us;
All I know to do is to ask.
We'll have to try to live on what we have left
Though it won't be an easy task.

It's amazing how You can still love us,
But You do, of that I have no doubt.
If we ask, will You please forgive us?
Reach down Your hand
And help us find a way out.

CALL ME

I wish I could convince you to get in touch
When life is going along quite happily.
It seems you only call when the road gets difficult,
And then you dump all your troubles on Me.

Now now, I'm not complaining; I understand.
I don't mind hearing your troubles at all.
I know life gets tough and you may shut others out.
You can come to Me and let down your every wall.

Remember I'm always here to lend a helping hand,
Listening to the bad but also to the good.
So call Me up sometime, anytime, and let's talk.

I love you;

You are My children;

I really wish you would.

DRIVING…THINKING…

The mountains stand quietly
As I drive by in the night.
My eyes grow heavy
As the evening wears on.

Moonlight helps show the way
Through most of the journey
Though pesky bits of fog
Reduce the moon's assist.

A day lacking in success
Clouds my mind as I drive
Just as the fog
Clouds the lines in the road.

My life is very much like this road…

I think I know where I'm going

But pesky bits of fog hinder progress

And I'm getting a bit road crazy.

THAT BOY

Dear boy,
It's hard to watch you cry
As you hide in your room,
Recovering from harsh words.

You were only trying to be yourself,
Find your way,
Be creative.
You didn't deserve that.

You need to know
You did nothing wrong.
It was his problem, his blindness,
Not yours.

You're a good boy,
A creative boy,
And you'll have many more chances
To be you.

I know you want to be angry
And speak what's on your mind.
And I know why you can't.
It's awful to be so gagged.

Dry your tears,
And don't lose hope.
Please don't let him
Hold you back.

You did nothing wrong.
You're a good boy.
Keep feeling what you feel.

It will all be worth it some day

When you grow up

And become me.

COMING FULL CIRCLE, ON A ROLLER COASTER

Have you ever wanted to have a do-over? Or maybe just get to revisit something, take another crack at it? Sometimes it happens...

In June of 1971, a new theme park called Six Flags Over Mid-America opened in the small town of Pacific, Missouri, near St. Louis. Watching the commercials for the park on television, my six-year-old mind spun wildly over the prospect of riding and seeing everything. Six Flags boasted several rides, including old-fashioned cars, a log flume ride, river adventure ride, plus petting zoos, a train that went around the entire park, and a roller coaster.

The next month, my parents planned one of our rare summer vacations, this time a trip to St. Louis. We planned to stay at a Howard Johnson's motel, which was terribly exciting to me, and the agenda included trips to several area attractions, a St. Louis Cardinals baseball game, and a day at Six Flags. I couldn't wait to see the new amusement park.

Driving up Interstate 44 in our station wagon, my siblings and I bounced around the car like caged monkeys. My sister Debbie, age 10, sat in the back seat and occupied her time by counting all the big trucks she saw. My brother Doug, 9, joined me in crawling into the back of the station wagon to wave at cars and trucks that passed us, as well as watch the landscape that passed by at a high rate of speed. As we neared the town of Pacific, we heard mom say that we should be passing Six Flags any time, so I plastered my face to the window in hopes of being the first to see the magical park. Within minutes, after passing a large hill, Six Flags came into view.

Instantaneously losing all my six-year-old senses, I screamed, "There it is!"

Little did I know, just before I screamed "there it is!"

Debbie spied several trucks travelling together and busied herself counting them. As soon as I yelled, she let out a grunt of disgust.

"Timmy you made me lose count!!! I've been counting since we left Springfield, and now I've lost track!"

I barely heard her as I looked out the window at the amusement park, nestled in a valley surrounded on three sides by looming tree-covered hills, with a large wooden water tower that said "Six Flags" on the side. Mom reminded us that we had other things to see on this trip, and that Six Flags was a few of days away. So Doug and I settled back into waving at cars as my sister sat in the seat, arms folded, angry that I made her lose count of the number of trucks she saw on the trip.

We visited the park on Monday of our vacation week, and I was wound up tighter than an eight-day clock. I'm not sure of the order in which we rode the rides, but knowing my family, we probably had an orderly approach to it. Dad bought a map of the park, which he, Mom and Debbie studied. On that old original map from that day, the rides we rode have an "X" on them, presumably noted by Mom, as she wrote the date on the map as well. There is one ride that has a big X on it, The River King Mine Train, of particular interest. It was the park's one and only roller coaster at the time.

In my memory, I do not recall if I watched the people on the ride before getting on, but I know I begged Dad to let me ride it, to which he agreed. In looking back on the event, I have to believe that by its name, I must have thought it was a train ride through a mine, and I must not have known it was a roller coaster, nor was I aware of how such a ride felt.

I recall that once we got into the building where the line started for the ride, I smelled the hot hydraulic fluid used to operate the ride's brakes and got a sense of foreboding. I grabbed Dad's hand as we wound our way through the line. My heat began to thump as I crawled into the car, followed by Dad. As the ride attendant locked the lap bar down over me, I began to wonder if picking this ride had been a good idea. Then once the ride started and we made a couple of sharp turns, I turned to Dad with a wild look in my eyes and told him I wanted to get off the ride. Of course at that point there was nothing anyone could do, and Dad just chuckled and said, "I can't stop the ride. You said you wanted to get on this thing, so you just have to ride it out."

I remember squeezing the lap bar, desperately holding on as my pleadings turned into a full-blown screaming and crying fit, horrified that I was stuck riding what seemed at the time to be a terrifying twisting journey into the gates of hell. Up hills, down hills, twisting left then right, I screamed and cried through the whole thing, yelling "Daddy make it stop". The last drop on the ride was the steepest, and I recall wailing through the whole thing and all the way into the station when it was done.

Mortified, Dad didn't care to ride anything else with me. I'm pretty sure he pawned me off on Mom at that point, and rode more adventurous rides with my older brother and sister.

Unfortunately from that day on, I found myself scared of riding roller coasters. Convinced that they were terrible things, I refused to ride anything that closely resembled one. Even at Silver Dollar City, an amusement park near Branson, Missouri, where in 1972 an indoor coaster called Fire in the Hole opened, it took a long time for me to agree to ride it, and even then I didn't enjoy it, but closed my eyes and got through it.

In 1973, another amusement park opened, this time near Kansas City, called Worlds of Fun. It had a few roller coasters when it opened, and when we went there a year or two later, I refused to ride the coasters, subjecting myself to the kiddie rides with my younger sister.

I stayed safely away from all roller coasters (except the occasional ride on Fire in the Hole) until age 15, when my brother Doug decided to take the situation into his own hands. The family planned to go to Kansas City again that summer, and the trip included a return visit to Worlds of Fun, which now boasted a new coaster called The Orient Express, and it had four loops in it. Doug said, "I'm going to break you of your fear of roller coasters. I want to ride The Orient Express, and YOU are going to ride it with me."

To put it mildly, the whole idea scared the living crap out of me. I woke up that morning, fearful but a bit excited, because I didn't know how Doug was going to get me to enjoy coasters, and whether or not it was really going to work. When we got to the park, Mom and Dad took Kathy to let her on some kiddie rides, so Doug and I were on our own for the great coaster adventure.

We started out on a small wild mouse roller coaster, called the Schussboomer. A zippy little ride, it had one big dip at the first, then lots of little dips and quick turns. I tried desperately to enjoy myself on that first ride, but in the end I was still unhappy about the experience. After getting off the ride, Doug turned to me and said, "I figured out what your problem is. You're fighting it. You're pulling back on the lap bar, trying to not go down the hill. Just lean into it and ride it down and try to enjoy yourself. And keep your eyes open!! Quit fighting it. Let's ride it again."

So we got back in line and we rode it again, and this time I tried to not fight it and ride it down... and I kept my eyes open. It worked! I actually enjoyed it more! So we rode it one more time, and I was a changed man, yelling and laughing as we zipped around in our little car.

With that little victory in our pocket, we moved on to another roller coaster, the Zambezi Zinger. A neat little speed racer type steel coaster built into a grove of trees, the Zambezi had a series of two-seat cars in which the riders were positioned one in front of the other. The train looped up a circular track several times before levelling out about fifty feet above the ground, then went down several dips and included lots of twists and turns. As Doug and I boarded the ride, he got on first to take the rear position, and I sat down in front of him. I noticed there were no lap bars or other restraints, just side bars to hold. Once we were going and winding through the trees at high speeds, I noticed how incredibly smooth the ride was. I loved it, and we rode it several of times.

After those rides on the Zambezi Zinger, Doug grinned and said, "Ok, you've enjoyed those two. Now let's hit the Orient Express."

Terrified, I agreed. We made our way across the park and got in line, picking a loading lane where we would be seated safely in the middle of the train. As we stood there in the building waiting to ride, I became aware of a smell: that old familiar smell of hot hydraulic fluid, and instantly my brain slipped back to that fearful day at Six Flags. With heart pounding, I took my seat and pulled the harness down over my head and locked it in place. The train slowly pulled out of the station, and there was no turning back.

The train lurched as the chain grabbed us, and we began to climb the highest coaster hill that I had ever ridden. The coaster dragged riders to a height over 115 feet in the air and it felt like we would never get there. My heart pounded and I seriously began to question Doug's sanity as he yelled and hollered on the way up. Once at the top, as we quickly rounded a curve, I looked down to see how high we were, and how steep that first dip looked. Doug laughed and said, "Holy shit, here we go!" Before I could take another breath, we went over the edge and began careening down that huge dive. I couldn't believe how it felt to fly down that hill, then suddenly loop upside down, not just once, but four times! The end of the ride had two tight spirals which brought the train to speeds up to 60 miles per hour. Certain I was flying, I held on tight, yelling all the way. By the time I got off the ride, I was laughing, yelling, whooping and hollering, as I felt I had tackled not only my fear of roller coasters, but had just experienced one of the wildest coasters in existence at that time.

The rest of the day we rode all three coasters several more times each. That night as I tried to drift off in my sleeping bag, I discovered my equilibrium was completely messed up from riding all those coasters. I spent the whole night feeling like I was going downhill and turning sharp corners.

Over the 33 years since that day, there have been many roller coaster rides, all of them thoroughly enjoyed. Sadly, none of the three coasters Doug and I rode that day at Worlds of Fun still exist, however they have been replaced by bigger and wilder coasters, which I am happy to have ridden. But in the back of my mind, I've never forgotten that fateful day in 1971, when at the tender age of six, I got scared on my first roller coaster ride. I've always thought about that ride, and how interesting it would be to ride that coaster again if it happened to still exist at Six Flags. Then in 2013, a full 42 years after that first ride, I finally had the opportunity.

I drove to Six Flags with my sons Kevin and Corey, and Kevin's girlfriend Cecily. We picked a terribly hot and sticky day for the excursion, but I could barely contain my excitement to once again be at the park, to see what had changed over the years. Plus I was anxious to go tripping down memory lane with some of the rides I recalled from all those years ago.

Naturally the park changed a lot over 42 years. More roller coasters occupied the place, and many of the old rides I recalled were long gone. One boat ride, known in 1971 as Injun Joe's Cave (with a nod to Mark Twain's books) had been converted to a Scooby Doo ride, but the old boats employed in 1971 were still in use, with a few modifications.

I looked at the park map when we got there, and noticed that they had a roller coaster with the same name as the one I recalled, the River King Mine Train, and it was in the general area that I remembered. After riding several rides, we made our way over to the old coaster. I looked at the information sign outside the entrance to the ride, and sure enough, it was the same old original ride. I couldn't wait to climb on and ride the old coaster that scared me so badly 42 years prior.

We took our places in line to ride in the middle of the train, which seemed like a smart choice, and Corey rode with me while Kevin and Cecily rode in the seat behind us. Climbing into the cars, I noticed that when the lap bar was pulled down, it fit tightly across my stomach. Since I'm considerably more stout than Corey, the bar was not down so tight on him, and I wondered if the same thing happened to me, since at six years old I would not have been as sturdy as Dad, so the bar was probably pretty loose and I had lots of room to flop around. That may have contributed to my fear back in 1971.

I also became aware once again of the smell of hydraulic fluid, that same smell I noticed as a little boy, and again on the Orient Express. I smiled to myself, remembering how foreboding it smelled when I was young.

My heart thumping as the train pulled out of the station, I was anxious to experience the ride again. We took a quick dip and a fast turn around a corner immediately upon leaving the station, and it was most likely at that point when I was six that I discovered this ride was more than I had bargained for. I told Corey, "I bet this point is where I told Dad I wanted off the ride."

Riding through the rest of the little coaster, I chuckled and laughed as we twisted through the trees and bounced up and down. The twists were tight, tighter than expected for an old steel coaster. And the last dip took place in total darkness as if you are down in a mine. I remembered that last dip to be the place where I screamed the loudest when I was six, but didn't remember it being dark there.

Pulling back into the station and laughing at how fun that old coaster ride was, I felt a special contentment deep down inside, knowing that I got to come full circle in my lifetime experiences of riding roller coasters. After 42 years, I got to experience once again a ride that had terrified me at a tender, vulnerable age. And even better, I got to experience it with three of my favorite people, my kids. They knew the story, and I think they were happy to see the old man get to experience such a thing.

    Walking away from the ride, I couldn't help but think about that six-year-old version of me. I wanted so badly to go back in time and grab that little guy, hold onto him and tell him it's ok to be scared, but to give the ride another shot, and that I would ride it with him this time.

A FEW PARTING THOUGHTS

Can you hear me in my final hour
As I lie here trying to breathe with all my power?
Can you feel the chill within this room
As I work my way back to Heaven's womb;
And can you hear the angels sing?
Oh, come now, don't cry about this thing

Called Death. It's really quite peaceful, you know,
Like the curtain going down on the final show.
This is the last act, and to you I leave
All my love. Oh please don't grieve
Because I'll be with you, you know I will.
Memories of me will live on still.

Come lay your cool cloth on me, dear Death,
As now I prepare to take my last breath.

Dry your tears now, put a smile on your face.
At last I'm going to that special place.
I hope you know I love you, because I do.
The sky must be clearing, because I can see through

The clouds...

My maternal grandfather, Earl Moore, was quite a character, to say the least. He had a sharp sense of humor, combined with a dry wit, and half the time you never knew whether he was serious or not. One thing is for certain, he enjoyed having laughter around him. By the time I reached my middle teen years, I began to really understand his sense of humor and appreciate him as a grandfather. He funneled some spending money my way if I did some basic "chores", which usually amounted to very little work. In his mind, I believe, it was all about making me earn it. He liked sharing in the simple things of life, like sitting on the front porch of his nice mobile home and waving at the traffic that went by, smelling approaching rain in a nice breeze, and the value of silence when there was nothing to say.

After Grandma died in 1986, I spent a lot of time contemplating and writing about death, and it bothered me that someday I would lose Grandpa as well. So I decided to write about how I felt about him, and the memories I had of him, if he were to die suddenly. Even though he was not the type to express or deal with emotions freely, I wanted him to know how I felt about him. So after writing this, the next time I saw him I read this poem to him. I didn't want another visit to go by without him knowing how important he was to me. After I finished reading it to him, he didn't say anything. He just smiled.

Fortunately, I got to enjoy him for an additional nine years. He died suddenly in 1995, four months after my mother (his daughter) died unexpectedly. I am thankful to have video recordings of him, especially footage of him with my sons, who were age two and four when he died. They only know him from what I have told them, and the treasured video footage.

I'm still glad I got to share this with him back in 1986...

GRANDPA

I have to say goodbye to you now
Though I really don't want to.
You've been such a good friend and we've had lots of fun,
Just you and I.

We've talked a lot about my classes,
And the technical things I have learned.
I've appreciated you wanting to know what's going on,
Like how many credit hours I've earned.

We've gone to Campbell Point, checked on the dock,
And taken boat rides by the score.
I swear Table Rock is the only lake I've ever known
Thanks to you, Mr. Moore.

We've also had some rough times, been through hell
At a hospital in Berryville,
Sitting in recliners, keeping vigil over Grandma,
Saying things I'll never tell.

Had lots of steaks at the Shell Knob Cafe,
Breakfast at Ginny's, Cozy's chicken, too,
Down in God's country, your place the Villa;
Some wonderful memories of you.

We've had some fun drinking beer,
Providing commentary for baseball games.

Now that you're gone, life feels strange.
It will never be the same.

You gave me your love in an indirect way,
Showed concern, showed you care;
I'll never forget how much you've meant to me,
I think about you everywhere.

You've been a great source of inspiration,
Gave me a push when I needed a shove.
Now that you're headed to that world beyond,
Please look down on me from above.

I send you now to that comfortable place
And I hope your back doesn't hurt anymore.
Let's keep in touch until once again
I can knock on your front door.

And Earl,

As you've always said:

Watch the traffic.

REQUIEM

Heavenly cherub –

Your song of life
Resonates
Through my soul.

I

Your flesh,
Your blood,
Remain
To listen to the echo
And continue the song,
Carrying on
Its many stanzas.

I wish to sing
As the Bachian pipes
Sad,
Low,
Driven.

Yet such must not be.

I

Must be strong

As a remaining singer
In a choir
Minus one.

My great-aunt Dora "Aunt Doty" Franklin was the family historian on my father's side. A sweet, frail, tiny lady, she welcomed all who graced her doorstep and was known in genealogy circles across the country as a wonderful, knowledgeable person. As my genealogy mentor, she gave me the inspiration and building blocks to continue researching my family history.

And then, there were the sugar cookies. "Aunt Doty's Sugar Cookies", they were called. I didn't know there could ever be any other sugar cookies on the planet. She always had some in a cookie jar; always. Time of year didn't matter, time of day didn't matter, the cookies were there and you were more than welcome to as many as you could eat.

Honored to deliver her eulogy when she died in 1999, I couldn't resist taking a moment to offer a final tribute to her:

ODE TO AUNT DOTY

Pretty in her checkered dress,
She finally reaches the door.
Her eyes light up as she recognizes you
And her greeting is a hug and a kiss on the cheek.

With feeble legs and little steps
She guides you to the couch.
Always happy to sit and talk,
And show off her latest pictures.

A phone call may for a moment interrupt,
But you strain to hear her sweet "Hello!"
And you cannot help but smile a bit
As she chats.

Am I Doug or am I Tim?
We usually get around to that.
Then we settle in to tales of old
And you get to watch her mind spin.

Spin as she recalls Uncle Pete and the farm
And her days as a young girl.
And beyond all that, she knows the tales,
And then the papers come out.

She is the Bookkeeper.

She gave me my first pieces of the Great Puzzle.
She showed me how to begin.
And she showed me where to begin:
In my heart.

Aunt Doty, thank you for your time.
Thank you for the pieces to the Great Puzzle.
Thank you for the open door and the sugar cookies
And thank you for your love.

And tell Pete we said hello…

This next poem is a style that I refer to as a "frantic poem". There is very little punctuation in this poem, and it's completely intentional.

My intent is for the reader to read each stanza without taking a breath until reaching a period. The idea is to read it as if a frantic person is speaking it.

I wrote this one while I was attending the University of Missouri – Rolla, now known as the Missouri University of Science and Technology. It is an engineering school, which is a demanding learning environment. Near my apartment a couple of blocks from campus, a microwave tower rose about 200 feet above the neighborhood, and was surrounded by barbed wire fence. A legend circulated around campus that the reason the fence encircled the tower was because very intelligent students, who had never before received a score below an A on any homework or test, would climb the tower and jump to their deaths because they got a C on a test.

I often wondered whether or not the legend was true. One night I began to imagine what it would be like to be the roommate of one such student, who would choose to end their life because of a bad grade. I thought about coming home to an apartment full of police, learning my roommate had shot himself in the bathroom, and trying to talk to the police amidst my upset and grief, pacing, crying, breathing hard, etc. After a few iterations, this is what came out…

I Quit

You live with someone for a couple of years
And have a few laughs over a few thousand beers
And you brace the guy up and help dry his tears
And he goes and pulls something like this.

We swear to always be best of friends
And even resolve time and again
To defend each other to the bitter end
In the midst of this single - life bliss.

Yeah, right.

He picks up the Playboys he never actually read
And places them neatly in a box on my bed
And goes in the john and puts a bullet through his head--
There was obviously something I missed.

He seemed to be alright
And laughed a lot last night
But somewhere in the middle of this Fight
His mind said, "I quit."

Damn.

I was very close to my maternal grandmother, Mary Catherine (Hays) Moore. She came to visit often, usually staying for a few days. I have many wonderful memories of her. I couldn't walk by without giving her a kiss, and she usually raised her arthritic fingers to my chin to give me a quick pinch with a wink. Another memory of Grandma that stands out in my mind is her phrase "Never fear, Grandma's here!" We used to kid her a lot about it, and it used to drive Mom nuts.

Grandma passed away in 1986, during my third year of college. Diagnosed with cancer all over her body, she left us just six short weeks after prognosis. She chose to die at her home in Shell Knob rather than the hospital. I was standing in the room, looking into her eyes as she was pronounced dead, then later helped load her into the hearse. It had a profound effect on me.

We typically never think to tell the people we love just how much we care until it is too late. We say terrible things about them while they are alive, then curse ourselves for saying those things after they are gone.

Shortly after her death, I felt Grandma speaking to me as I drove back to college. These are the words I felt…

NEVER FEAR

"When everything comes crashing down around you,
Never fear.
When you feel that all your friends have left you,
Never fear;

The road of life is tough and long
And it's not always easy to be strong;

But there will always be one who loves You,
        Never fear."

Though words aren't always spoken,
Feelings not always shared,
I know how much she loved me.
She showed how much she cared.
When life gets tough and I can't go on
I'll look to the heavens and
Dear Catherine I will hear—

"It's okay
Never fear
I'm right here..."

REFLECTIONS

You died in my arms tonight
And I cannot explain why
There's no sorrow or pain.
Did you really go and die?

Funny, I didn't feel anything,
I haven't for a long time.
There have been enough rips and tears
To destroy this heart of mine.

When cut, I bleed now
A dark stagnant blood.
A heart of stone will not work,
Its pump clogged with mud.

Mud, because I learned alas
That I did not know of love.
This angered and frightened me,
And I cried to God above,

"Help me please to learn soon
Of the beautiful feelings to share.
I'm still young, but old enough
To learn to love and care."

My mistakes have been many
And my victories very few
And I've realized my biggest mistake
Was ever thinking that I knew

What real love is
Or was, or could be.
So I built a wall around my heart
And it encircled me.

My wall was made of brick and steel,
Mortar of blood and fire.
No one could get in to hurt me.
Did I mention the wire?

An electric line of current
Driven by the charge
Of my once-strong physical desires,
Destroyed by a barrage

Of idle offers and teasing,
And ignoring my wants and needs.
I ignored the pain as long as I could
And silenced my soul's pleas.

Now my organs have ceased to exist,
Those outer and within.
Love is not alive within me,
And caring is a sin.

So here you lie, dead in my arms,
And I cannot say but this;
That I hope soon Death, too, will come to me
And allow me silent bliss.

In December of 1994, a legend in country music passed from this earth: Si Siman. You may have never heard his name, but the country music industry was most certainly influenced by him. He discovered and promoted singers and musicians like Brenda Lee, Porter Wagoner, and Chet Atkins. He also played a key role in the creation of the Ozark Jubilee, a show televised from Springfield, Missouri in the 1950s. He knew my parents from their involvement in the local music scene, and his daughter, Jaynie (Siman) Chowning, was good friends with my mother. Additionally I worked with Jaynie and her husband Randall during the 1990s at a manufacturing facility in Springfield.

I visited with Si just before his death, asking him about country singer and movie star Tex Ritter, as he and Tex were good friends. He was eager to offer any information he had, and was very kind as we visited. He died after a long illness in mid-December of '94, and it bothered me, especially since I had just recently talked with him. So the night before his funeral, I decided I needed to write about it…

A Note to Si

I sit alone tonight, not knowing what to do
So with pen in hand, I pay tribute to you.

The sun beamed so on your musical heart
And you shared your love through the art.

You will long be known for your Jubilee,
A part of your life that ties to mine.

You knew my father, he and his twin,

My mother as well was glad to call you friend.

When I shook your hand earlier this year,
I felt your strength, a tingle right here.

And even in your illness, you took interest in my quest
To trace my family heritage. You were simply the best.

And there are those who can better testify
And tell of the glories of your musical life.

Chet, Brenda and Porter freely give credit due
To the advances their careers made, thanks to you.

We're all united in grief, not knowing what to do
As we sit, Kleenex in hand, and fondly remember you.

But I must smile to myself as I see you shake hands
As Lefty and Mr. Acuff welcome you to the Promised Land.

Let us now breathe deeply, turn on the lights
As we all miss you this December night.

May our sorrow soon pass, and we grieve no more.
Then we'll all sit together and share Si Siman stories.

THE BRIDGE

Barely standing, grasping the ropes, I struggle to breathe in the cold wet air. My legs tremble, knees wanting to buckle, as I fight the pain in my head.

And this bridge keeps moving.

I take a meek step forward, squinting through the fog in hopes of catching a glimpse of something before me, some indication of where I am, where I've been… or how high I am above any objects below…

The pain in my head, behind my eyes, tortures me as if something sinister is holding a raw nerve with a pair of tweezers and squeezing it with every thump of my pounding heart. Thump. Squeeze. Thump. Squeeze. Thump. Squeeze.

Inching forward, I hear screaming through the mist. It comes from everywhere, nowhere, above and below. Looking behind me does no good. There is only forward, or at least, I think so…

Another step, and the boards, wet and almost mossy under my bare feet, make unsettling squishing sounds, as if their saturation has weakened them beyond the capacity to support my weight. I don't want to fall. Please don't let me fall.

Thump. Squeeze. Thump. Squeeze.

I wish I could hear something. No, not the screams again. I want to hear something else, anything else. Running water, a breeze through tree limbs, the buzz of a mosquito just before it bites my ear. Anything. Ichabod Crane at least had the sound of his horse's hooves as he ventured into the dark, sinister woods. I want to hear something.

A chill runs up my spine as I become aware of someone's hot breath on the back of my neck. I turn quickly to face the specter, rocking the bridge wildly.

No one is there.

And it's getting darker.
Thump. Squeeze. Thump. Squeeze.

I turn back around and tighten my grip on the ropes.

Another scream blasts through the mist, swimming around me in the dank air, and I want to cover my ears…

But I don't dare let go of the ropes…

The smell of Death wafts into my nostrils, but I know not from where. Over what do I cross? What horrors surely await me below if only I could see them? Am I perilously traversing over some field where the dead lay in silence? Is it some death-filled lake teeming with destroyed wildlife, their spoiled bodies floating with glassed-over eyes seeing past me into nothingness? Or am I smelling what's left of those who tried to cross this bridge before me?

Thump. Squeeze. Thump. Squeeze.

The board below my right foot snaps under my weight. My left foot slips on its wet plank, and I almost lose my grip. I pull myself forward quickly, to get away from the spot. How many more boards will snap beneath me?

Thump. Squeeze. Thump. Squeeze.

It's getting darker. Still no sound, save for the wretched screams that pierce the fog, live within the fog, surround me like the fog. I'll take the silence if the screams will stop.

I continue to move forward, knowing not where I'm going, nor where I've been, nor why I'm here. The pain in my head clouds my thinking, and my entire world has collapsed into this tiny, damp, fog-enshrouded place, with each step I take.

Thump. Squeeze. Thump. Squeeze. Thump. Squeeze.

Screams once again pierce the fog, like a clap of thunder from a nearby lightning strike. They don't stop, but continue deliriously in wail after wail after wail, with barely a breath taken between. The screams become more hoarse, more desperate, more exhausted, more horrified…

My throat burns, I cough hard, doubling over, struggling to catch my breath.

I hear another scream and in the horror of that moment, I recognize its source… it's coming from within me. They've all been from me.

Thump. Squeeze.

I scream again, owning my anguish, letting it out with all that is within me.

Thump. Squeeze.

I stand now silent, exhausted, panting.

Thump. Squeeze.

The light wanes and fog surrounds me.

Thump. Squeeze.

My grip on the ropes tightens.

Thump. Squeeze.

Thump. Squeeze.

Thump. Squeeze.

With the last glimmer of daylight, the fog suddenly clears, and I can see everything around me, above me, below me…

Oh shit…

A One-sided Chat with the Dragon

So that's enough about you, let's talk about me...

I dwell in darkness; I like all things black
But I look quite good in candlelight,
Don't you agree?

My social life is quite satisfying.
I have a reputation for holding intimate gatherings
That often draaaaag on into the night.

Ladies are usually dying to see me.

No, I did not choose this lifestyle...
Lifestyle, how amusing!
What was I saying?

Thank you, no, I did not choose this.
I had it, shall we say,
Shoved down my throat.

I'm definitely a night creature.
I choose to sleep during the day.
Exposure is bad for the skin.

Dear me, look at the time.
It appears to be getting late.
I'd guess you'd best be on your way--

Or would you like to stay—

Hang around for a while...

This is a rather horrifying piece, penned when I was deep in the throes of depression over many things, including the chill which had descended over my marriage. It is also the first of two poems in which I made reference to "The Dark Man". In my mind this represented everything evil and painful, and looked similar to Liam Neeson's character in the movie "Darkman", hence the name. Yet while Neeson's character was something resembling a flawed superhero, my Dark Man stayed in the shadows bringing evil, destruction and pain.

TWITCH

Ten sticks of dynamite
Strapped to my chest,
My finger twitches
As I caress the button.

Am I really in charge,
Calling the shots?
It feels like I'm strapped to a chair on a ride to death
And the Dark Man just released the brake.

I'm trying to make sense
Of this world of mine
And what became
Of the world which used to be.

A world of Love it was,
Where I meant as much to her
As she meant to me.
What a nice combination.

I thought it was supposed to be that way…
Now I live in another world
Where I am the Semi-Great Provider
And my duties numerous
Day after day after goddamn day.

There are two kids who don't know
I've got my finger on the button.
I'm not so sure
She can even see the dynamite...

Twitch...

LOSING IT

I don't want to hear that you love me.
I don't want to know that you care.

Don't touch me, I don't think I could take it.
Don't look at me, you over there.

I'm walking the edge of a razor blade,
Somewhere between Silence and Scream.

On one side there is peace and tranquility,
On the other, Insanity's eyes gleam.

You say, "What the hell is he talking about?"
And I answer, "I honestly don't know."

I want to believe none of this is really happening
And I keep repeating, "It's only a show."

Memorial Night

A blinding fog lies thick below the cliffs
As the wind blows, screaming past my ears,
Chilling me to the point of pain,
Punishing me for my late-night journey.

I pull my coat around me--
I fancy it provides strange protection
From what unknowns lie ahead –
But alas wool can only protect me from the cold,
Nothing else.

The road looks much different by day,
Always a bit steep and rocky,
Now so dark and deadly,
Full of night's creatures.

My lantern, fighting to stay alit,
Captures pairs of eyes, low to the ground,
Watching me.
From a distance they seem safe.
Even creatures that lurk about in the dark
Seem frightened this night.

I struggle to find sure footing
As I continue my trek upwards
To the familiar stone entrance,
Now coming into view.

Stopping at the worn wrought iron gate,
I neaten the fragrant bouquet,
Brought to this horrifying place
With my dearest in mind
In loving hope it may keep her warm.

I work my way to the familiar stone,
Though tonight's godless black
Casts hell's darkest shadow
Over even her grave.

Dropping to my knees,
I kneel by the cold granite,
Damp to the touch,
To sweep the leaves away
From her precious name.

"Lysette," I whisper
As I place my gift on the earth,
"Your love has returned to bid you well--
I hope you are comfortable."

Another gale comes screaming through the valley
As twigs snap behind me.
Is someone there?

The flame in my lantern surrenders to the wet gust,
Extinguished forever,
And I panic
As I am plunged into darkness.

Yet I know where I am,
My love lies beneath the soil before me.
I grieve, cry aloud, and ask the moonless sky,
"Why?!"

I must kiss the soil that entombs her delicate self,
As tears roll down my face
And drip onto the ground below me.

My pulse quickens, my mind races,
My body trembles
As in darkness I slowly lean toward the ground.

What madness is this? Am I dreaming?
As my lips, cold and wet, touch the mossy earth
My Lysette's face breaks through the earth
And our lips meet in a timeless kiss.

I blink quickly, lest my sleep continue
And this dream, this nightmare takes me.
Yet I am awake.
I realize to my horror
The nightmare is real!

Her gray wet hands and legs
Quickly break through the mound,
Around my neck her cold fingers crawl.
Her lengthy nails penetrate my skin
As her icy grip suddenly tightens.

Pull away I try. I cannot move!
My love, my sweet Lysette, undead,
Has me.

My eyes gaze upon Lysette's lifeless stare
As her teeth latch onto my bloodied lower lip.
My muscles strain, fighting against her pull
As tightly her legs wrap around me.

To scream I try, though who can come?
I am alone, with no one near this place
For many miles.
I am alone.

I must escape! I must break free!
Yet my every exertion is met with agony
As my love, my undead love,
Drives her nails deeper into my skin.

My futile resistance ends as my joints collapse
While she continues our painful kiss.
I let out a muffled cry as I'm slowly pulled down
To eternally join my lovely Lysette.

THE TERROR INSIDE

Welcome to the terror
Of this destructive mood.
Note the shadows which surround me.
I made them myself.

I writhe in the sticky web
As the spider sharpens her fangs.
I hear her laugh as she watches me
Further entangle myself.

In horror I watch as she looks my way
And begins her approach.
I feel her hot breath upon my neck
As her legs wrap around me.

Slowly, painfully she licks me,
Tasting me,
Testing me,
Preparing me as her meal.

If I thought it would help,
I would scream…

Wait, I'm already screaming.

I've been screaming for a long time…

The Mirror

I stood at the mirror to my soul,
And tried to decide if I liked what I saw.

"Take a look ...
Take a long look ..."

Did I feel comfortable
Looking at me
Like I fear others do?

Did I stand
Before myself
In silent judgment.

I gripped the chair,
Crutch of my stance.

Away from the mirror
At last I turned

And wept.

PURGATORY

Standing here in Purgatory
Where all is fog and darkness.
The icy wind chokes
As it screams down my throat
And I gasp for air.

I thought I heard a friendly voice
Calling through the fog,
Offering to guide me through
This awful place
And give me peace and comfort.

But it was just my mind
Making a fool of my heart,
For there was no one,
No one there at all.

The journey through
Must be made alone
With no exceptions.

This is the second poem which uses the imagery of The Dark Man. When my mother died suddenly in December of 1994, and subsequently several other family members and friends died in 1995, I spent many hours brooding and grieving over the loss of so many. The loss of Mom and my grandfather hit hard, and brought about another opportunity to write in an attempt to express the pain. It's short, but expressed everything I had to say in that moment.

GONE

The Dark Man took a knife
And quickly cut you from our life.

We stand as one, bleeding,
With no hope of blood receding.

No salve can ever hope to ease the pain
And we wonder if we will ever be the same.

ELEVATOR GIRL

I can't remember the first time I saw her.

She might have walked by the greeting card shop where I worked in high school. Or she might have caught my eye once when I dropped by the store where she worked. Whatever the circumstances, I had a crush on her. And I'm not really sure what caught my notice first. Was it her pretty red hair, or the cute little freckles that dotted the soft skin around her delicate nose? It could have been either one, but I'm guessing it was her eyes, big and sparkling. Any time our eyes met, I couldn't breathe.

She operated an old-fashioned elevator at a downtown women's clothing store next to the greeting card shop where I worked part time as a clerk. Mom worked there also, as a clerk.

The entire front of the card shop was glass, with the checkout station at the front, so I could easily see everyone who happened to walk by... including her. I didn't know how old she was, but she appeared to be a few years older than me. With adolescent hormones raging, I was completely spellbound by her.

One time (and one time only) I made the mistake of telling Mom how cute I thought the Elevator Girl was, and how much I would love to ask her out.

"No, you don't need to do that," Mom said, shaking her head emphatically, "She has lots of health problems. And besides, she wouldn't be interested in you anyway. Your dad doesn't make enough money and we live on the west side of town."

Mom hated it when I expressed interest in a girl, and always tried her best to destroy my confidence. The facts that we were poor and lived on the west side of town were her favorite jabs to use, although I never understood why it mattered how much money we had or why a girl should judge me based on our address. But that was it, I was forbidden to ask her out. The Elevator Girl became one of many girls I had to admire from a distance.

One chilly Saturday, while I was running the card shop by myself, I stepped out and walked next door to her store. There under the pretense of wanting to get a soda out of their machine, I really wanted to see my Elevator Girl, to see if she happened to be working that day.

The Junior Department was run by Mom's friend Penny, and they had a soda machine in their break area, near the changing rooms. Penny repeatedly told me that I was welcome to come get a drink any time. If no one was in the fitting rooms, I could go behind the counter and get a bottle myself. But if someone was trying on clothing, I could just give her my change and she would get the drink for me.

That particular day, a young lady was trying something on, so I gave my money to Penny and waited. I stood at the counter, looking around, and turned my head to the right, so that I could look for my redheaded Elevator Girl in the main section of the store.

The elevator door was open and I looked to see if she was perched on her wooden stool. It stood empty, and I wondered if she was taking a break.

Suddenly, there she was. She walked from the rear of the store toward the front, and when she was directly across from me in the aisle, she turned and looked in my direction.

Our eyes met.

Being a backward teenage boy, my first instinct was to look away. But I couldn't. I just stood there, looking at her, holding my breath.

She looked incredible, as always. I still remember how she looked as she walked across my field of vision in that split second, as if she moved in slow motion. Wearing a purple sweater over a white shirt, its collar and cuffs showing, her plaid wool skirt, full of soft purples and browns, flowed around her while she walked. Her chunky heeled boots made a lovely sound as she crossed the wood floor.

She continued looking at me for that brief moment she was in view in the doorway. Then, less than one second later, she was gone.

I quit holding my breath.

I was trembling as Penny came back around the corner with a bottle of orange soda. The whole experience had taken place in the span of less than five seconds. But even now, so many years later, each of those seconds is burned permanently in my mind. With soda in hand, I thanked Penny and walked back to the store, lost in recollection.

Our eyes had met.

Over time, I got to where I would wave at her any time she walked by the big plate glass windows at the front of the store. She always smiled and waved and kept walking. It drove me crazy. I so wanted to know her, spend time with her. Why did it matter that she had health problems? I wanted to get to know her. And I hoped that maybe she wouldn't care that I lived on the west side of town, and that my dad made less than $25,000 a year. Who knew, maybe her dad didn't make much money either.

She came in once on a Saturday, when I ran the store by myself. Springtime had arrived after a long dreary winter, and many people spent their lunch hour that day enjoying the warm sunshine. Someone somewhere outside cut themselves, and my Elevator Girl happened to be nearby. She ran into my store asking if I had a bandage. My fingers fumbled with the box that we kept under the counter for emergencies as I asked her what size she needed. She quickly said, "Medium is fine," so I fished one out. I longed to talk with her, but she was in too much of a hurry for small talk. Within seconds she was out the door and scooting across the square to attend to whomever had cut themselves.

She was right in front of me, and all we got to do was pick

out a bandage. Good lord.

One day, though, I actually rode in that elevator with her.

On this particular day, Mom needed me to go next door to pay a bill on her charge account. The billing department was on the second floor, so I had to take the elevator to get there. I walked next door and made my way through the Juniors Section, past the jewelry counter, and over to the elevator.

Her elevator.

With slightly trembling fingers, I stood at the door to the elevator and pressed the "up" button. I stood there waiting, listening to the vintage elevator slowly work its way down to the first floor. Then with a thump and a couple of loud rattling noises, the door slid open, an elderly lady came walking out, and there to the left on a stool sat the lovely elevator girl, looking at me.

I smiled, stepped in, and she closed the door.

Now was my chance. She was three feet away, and we were going to spend the next ten seconds together, just the two of us in that wood and steel box. I could say hi to her, ask her name, tell her mine. I might be able to make her laugh. Then later, after I paid Mom's bill, I would need to ride down again, another ten seconds together! And if I got really brave, I might even hold the door open and get another ten seconds when we got back down to the first floor.

But then I remembered what Mom said previously.

"She wouldn't be interested in you."

Why not? Maybe she would.

"You live on the west side and your dad makes less than $25,000 a year."

Why would that matter? What if her dad doesn't make much either? And we don't know where she lives. Maybe she wouldn't care what side of town I lived on.

But then again, maybe she was right. Maybe she wouldn't be interested. Maybe living on the west side of town and being poor made me less desirable, less attractive, less of a person.

Maybe this wasn't my chance at all. Perhaps I was just kidding myself.

I turned, looked in those pretty blue eyes, and spoke: "Second floor, please."

BREAKDOWN

I cried tonight,
I'm not sure why.
The walls closed in
And I wanted to die.

Life felt so good
For a day or two
But a few hours ago,
It began to undo

With talk of money,
Thoughts of school,
And all that is left,
All-nighters to pull.

I just can't take it;
I have done so well
At ignoring things,
Bouncing them off my shell.

But it's all too much
To deal with now.
Yet I've got to pick up
And dust off somehow.

I can't take the pressure
Of job search and class.
It will be so nice
To have a job at last.

I'm in no condition
To study now.
My fingers tremble
Under a sweaty brow.

My eyes fill with tears
As I realize I can't take the test
Despite confident guise.
It's just too much
For me to take.
A string stretches so far
Before it breaks.

Great timing...

I Lost

Time to again don the heavy armor
And protect my heart once more.
Time to grab this heavy shield
And carry it with me always.

Time to draw the sword once again
And fight
If I have the strength.

Hoped I did for one last battle
To gain the victory
And take home the prize
Of the fair maiden.

But too long I waited
To engage the enemy
And now find myself surrounded,
Cut off from retreat.

And the maiden is gone.

Another warrior rises,
More noble,
The better man.
He has taken her into his arms
And rides away with her.

I still can see them,
Barely.
I still hear them,
Barely,
But my name she does not call.

I have lost the maiden,
But the battle rages on.
I am not certain of the spoils of victory,
If victory is to be gained.

And know I shall to eternity
That I lost her
Over my own failure
To engage the enemy.

I was not the better man,
Nor will I ever be.

BREAKING THE HORSE

I am broken.

You have tied a rope around my neck
And have beaten me until I bleed
And did it all in the name of Control
And in the name of your needs.

Now gone is my spirit
Taken away
By idle offers and promises
And by leaving your love unspoken.

I began as a wild mustang,
Wild and ready to tackle all,
Take all,
Be all.

Yet I had a tender side
Capable of love,
Capable of dreams,
Capable of giving.

But you have beaten
All that out of me.

I am broken.
I have no more to give.

I can give you a ride,
But will feel nothing,
Nor will I feel loved.

I can work for you,
But will feel no satisfaction,
And will not feel appreciated.

I can cry for you.
I do that really well.

I am broken.

MAKING LOVE TO THE WOLF

I try to give this an honest attempt,
And I try to love you like I once did
But I can't help the way I feel--
Like I'm making love to the Wolf.

You're covered in sheepskin
And you look and feel soft and warm
But I've seen your teeth gnashing here and there
And I know what lies hidden...

And it terrifies me...

It's like sleeping with the enemy,
Waiting for the gun to be drawn
Or the knife pulled
From between the mattresses.

So go ahead and hurt me
That's what you truly enjoy--
It's not as if I can't see it coming.

My, what big teeth you have...

THE DOOR

I remember this place very well,
As I stood here many years ago.

I recall the door
And how dark and cold it was outside.
And it seemed warmer and lighter back inside.

I recall closing the door,
Turning around,
And staying where it was warm, familiar…

But the comfort didn't last long,
Not even a year
But I held on for many more
Through the loneliness.

Now I'm back at the door again,
Older,
Not wiser.

It's still cold and dark outside,
And it feels warm and light inside
Again.

But for how long?

To close the door,
And stay inside,
I must give up all I hope to find out there:

Light that lasts.
Warmth that lasts.
Love that lasts.

To walk through the door,
I must give up all I know
And jump.

I have stood at this door
For seven months now.

My hand is on the knob
And I am looking outside

And I am so scared.

Is anyone out there?

THOUGHTS OF BLEEDING

My dead soul lies bleeding
As I become an empty shell.
I yell more at my kids now
And remain distant.

I'm going through the motions,
Not trying to live,
But to survive
The fear and loneliness.

If I leave, I'll have nothing.
If I stay, I'll have nothing
Except a former lover.

WAVING EACH OTHER GOODNIGHT

Stop right there, dammit--
don't move a muscle.
I'm tired of coming to you,
expected to do it all.

I want you to stop for a moment
before you lie down
and give me some of your precious time
to feel loved.

I can't take another evening
like all the rest,
waving each other goodnight
with nothing passing between us.

Forgive me for the weakness
of needing affection.
I'm not just another damn man--
my soul cries for love.

I'm glad you're so tough
that you don't need anyone
but the rest of us need a little love
to get through the day.

Is it too much to ask
to be made love to?
I'd like to receive
once in a while.

The battle lines have been drawn,
the schedule of importance worked out:
First, the kids, then you--
I get what's left.

if anything.

Just because I hurt,
just because I have needs,
just because I need reassured,
don't think of me as weak.

Love me.
Reassure me.
Giving is not a sign of weakness.

No matter how strong I am,
no matter how good of a father I am,
I'm telling you this—

You've got a pretty damn good thing here,
but if I can't feel loved
I can't stay.

Connie

Do you remember your first crush? Of course you do. That first person to make you feel giddy and foolish, take your breath away just because they blinked. That first person to bring to the surface all those previously unknown feelings, strange and frightening, yet exhilarating. For me, it happened at the ripe old age of six.

My first crush was Connie, a girl in my 2nd grade class at Westport Elementary School in Springfield, Missouri. I don't recall when I first noticed her. I just know that once I noticed her, I couldn't get her out of my head. The tallest girl in the class, certainly taller than me, her black hair swirled around her cute round face of olive skin. I believed her to be of American Indian descent, with the most beautiful complexion, like soft smooth chocolate. Even as a little boy, I wanted to touch her face, softly run my fingers over her skin.

She wasn't skinny like the other girls in class. I realized she moved differently from the other long-armed, long-legged clumsy girls. I watched her run around the playground, and noticed how she moved. And I liked her boots. She wore soft-looking boots often, and they caught my attention.

Then one day, it all changed.

This particular day, Connie looked terribly sad. I found out that it was her last day at my school, as her family decided to move elsewhere, though I knew not why nor where. Her mother came to get her that afternoon, and Connie cried and cried, not wanting to leave. I remember watching her pack up all her things from her desk, tears streaming down her face, dripping off those soft cheeks that I wanted to touch, making little drops on her papers. She didn't bawl or make noise, just quietly wept as she packed her belongings with her mother's assistance.

I wanted to help. But then again, I didn't want her to leave. So I just sat and watched, aching.

She waved and said goodbye to everyone, tears still running down those cheeks that I imagined were so soft. I quietly said bye and waved and watched her walk out.

Right after she left, I happened to look in the closet where our coats hung and our lunchboxes sat in an orderly row, and I noticed her lunchbox still sitting there. She forgot to grab it!

I raised my hand and told my teacher, Mrs. Shannon, that Connie had forgotten her lunchbox. She told me to take it and run to the front door of the school to see if I could catch her.

Really? Me?

I jumped up from my chair, almost airborne, excited to get to do something for the girl I loved. I ran to the closet, grabbed her lunchbox, and took off out the classroom door at top speed.

It wasn't that far to get from Mrs. Shannon's room to the front door of the school, but at age six it felt like a marathon run. I ran as fast as I could, all the while hoping I would catch her, and she would see that I was her hero, and she would never leave. She'd be my girl, I just knew it.

I shoved open the huge wooden door and stepped out into the school yard. Looking around, I saw snow falling in huge wet flakes. Panting, I looked to my right, and there was no Connie. I quickly looked to my left, and there she was, in her oversized brown corduroy coat with the fur trim around the hood, and her pretty brown boots, walking with her mom to their car. I called out her name and began running toward her. Connie stopped and turned around to see me running with her lunchbox. Still crying, she walked toward me.

"You left your lunchbox, Connie," I said, holding it out to her.

She took the lunchbox, said, "Thank you Timmy" and

leaned over and kissed me on the cheek as one of her tears dripped onto my skin. She turned around, still crying, walked to her car and got in. Just like that, Connie was gone.

I stood there, in the falling snow, frozen in my tracks. I'm sure my mouth dropped open. She kissed me. I couldn't believe she kissed me. Connie, the pretty, tall girl in the boots, kissed me. And I was never going to see her again. I reached up and felt her teardrop on my cheek.

After a few seconds I started breathing again. I turned around and slowly walked back into the school as the snow fell around me and the world silenced to a hush. Before closing that big wooden door, I turned around one more time to look to where Connie's mom's car had been, to see if maybe she came back. She didn't.

I have no photograph of Connie, and I never even knew her last name. But even after all these years, I'm still haunted by the memory of standing there in the cold air, big wet snowflakes falling around me, feeling her sad teardrop still on my cheek where she kissed me, and watching her walk away.

I would go on to have countless crushes on countless girls (and women). Many have faded into nameless and even faceless patches of memory. But even now, there's a certain kind of silence during snow that takes me back to that day and my first crush.

ALONE ON VALENTINE'S DAY (AGAIN)

Why can't lovers be friends
And friends be lovers,
And why do people have to live
One without the other?

I feel the need to hold Someone,
To feel her loving touch;
I want to be held tenderly by her
And know that she cares so much.

I spent tonight alone, staring at the phone,
Waiting for that Someone to call.
The call never came, despite whispering her name,
What fate did I befall?

A night which lovers and florists celebrate,
A night of holding hands and kissing.
Yet I spent the night at odds with myself,
Thinking of the life I was missing.

Yes, I'm free to come and go as I please
And free to spend all night on the phone,
But I'm also free to spend every holiday
Completely alone.

Sorry, that's not living.

During my fourth year of college, I developed a routine for study that was rather unusual, but it worked for me. Each night after dinner, I left my apartment and headed to a building called the University Center. Filled with tables and chairs, a former lunch room served as the perfect quiet place to study. Then, at 10:00, a buddy and I walked over to The Cavern, a basement bar about a block away. We each drank exactly one longneck of Bud Light and played exactly one game of pinball, then headed over to the Denny's restaurant to continue our studies. At midnight, we took a break, ate a bite (or two), then continued studying until about 2:00 a.m.

My writing flourished at this time, and often I took a break from studying to write little ditties and quick thoughts that stuck in my mind. I decided to group those short pieces into this collection of random thoughts.

COFFEE AT DENNY'S – A COLLECTION

Release my wings and let me fly.
If I remain, will surely die.
Let there be no remorse, don't cry.
Just let you go...

~

I'm a rhesus monkey...
You watch me,
You analyze me.
You're fascinated by what you see.
Please stop.
Just love me...

~

I'm going through the speed zone in your heart.
There's not much can be done on my part.
You're the cop;
You're in charge.
Do I get a ticket?

~

You looked so good.
You felt so good.
Love felt so good.
Yet it wasn't quite good enough,
Not good enough for me.
So what makes me so goddamn special?

~

There's got to be an equation
That governs love.
This crap can't all be happening
Just by chance.
Where's my calculator?

~

The wind carries your soft fragrance
And allows the leaves to join me
In whispering your name...

~

The eternal light of my inner world,
I look upon this special girl
Becoming woman while I'm away...
I love you, sis.

~

So by and by
Just let me die,
And as I fly,
Tell me—

Did I do okay?

~

So now what do I do?
I'm afraid to move,
My walls are down.
I have this fear
Of looking like a clown
Again.

~

You laughed while I wept
You used as I kept
You seemed so adept;
So while am I still alive?
And why are you dead?

~

Why does it have to hurt to say "I Love You"
Why does it have to hurt to say "I Care"
How much longer must my heart lie dead
Without its love to share...

~

A heavy fog drops over the city
As I try to concentrate on my work.

My mind trails off to thoughts of you
And I smile to myself.

~

In the silence I find your eyes speak to me
More clearly than any spoken word
And they tell me of the love you have for me;
The most beautiful sounds I've never heard.

~

How I long to see you again.
On me you have cast a great spell.
To touch you now would be heaven.
To be without you now is Hell.

~

Do the things you know I must see;
Wear the things which make me wild;
Seduce me
And I shake inside...

~

You make me happy.
You make me smile.
I look forward to our meetings.
Let's talk for a while.
I can tell you that I love you
Because you know what I mean.
You are my friend.
You are my brother.

~~~

HARDENING THE HEART

Of things that are desired of life & love,
Those burnings which keep one awake,
Make one's soul and heart but ache,
Driving to the edge of madness.

If they are not given freely and willingly,
With glad heart and open spirit,
By the one from which they are desired,

Then they no longer keep one awake,
They no longer make one's soul and heart ache,
They no longer drive one to the edge of madness.
Rather they harden the heart,
And make the one who was once desired
No longer so.

It Ends Now

She stood with her toes in the wet sand
On the beach of an inlet of Maine.
A single tear ran down her sad cheek
As she knew life would never be the same.

It had to change…

No more rejection, no more nights
Awake for hours, longing to be held.
"The legacy ends," she whispered to herself
As she leaned over to pick up a shell.

Couples strolled nearby hand-in-hand
And she thought "I wish that was me
With someone special, someone loving."
She turned and looked longingly at the sea.

The shell in her hand, wind in her hair,
And the smell of sea air in her soul,
She turned and confidently walked back to the cabin,
Ready for the next chapter in her life to unfold.

"Time to take back my life," she said

As she reached for the door…

HEADPHONES

Speak to me, music of the night.
Ease my troubled soul.
Help me to forget the issues of the day---
I must rest.

Use your upbeat rhythms and guitar solos
To make my spirit soar.
Sing the words of my life.
Speak to me...

How I wish I could create music
As you so easily do.
My salvation is my pencil
(And its worn eraser).

Thank you for keeping me company
Through my long and lonely evenings.

NIGHT LOVE

I awaken and see you next to me
In a world of shadows, deep blue.
Two a.m. reads the clock on the wall
And sleepily I lie looking at you.

In the midst of your sleep and breath, slow and deep,
Your beauty shines as a glow in the night.
Your delicious form I see outlined perfectly
And I smile as I contemplate the sight.

My eyes, they begin to dim again
As my hand edges closer to thee.
I wish to touch the soft skin of your arm
But instead drift off to another sleep.

Welcome back, my friend Slumber,
As I slowly go under,
And my last sight before I sleep is her.

I awaken with a moan as I find myself alone;
You're not here, and what's worse, you never were.

THE GAME

December 30, 1964: Batter up!

I started out playing whiffle ball
With a plastic bat
And a plastic ball which didn't hurt much
When a wild pitch came in.

I didn't connect with the ball very often
But not that many pitches were thrown.
I spent more time fielding.

I eventually evolved to softball.
I needed a bigger bat, made of wood,
And I needed to connect
A little more often than before.

The ball was more solid,
The pitchers were better,
And my times at bat
Outnumbered the moments spent fielding.

I did field occasionally, though,
But needed a glove.
Catching at times proved painful.

Now I'm playing baseball
And hardly ever field.
I spend most of my times at bat,
Swinging at fast pitches.
And the damn ball is even smaller.

It seems that just when
I've got the pitcher figured out
And can prepare to swing

He throws a curve ball,
And I've got another strike against me.
Technically, none of us are supposed
To have more than three
But I've lost count—

I should have been out a long time ago.

IF I COULD FEEL YOUR LOVE

If I could feel your love,
I wouldn't be so afraid
Of everything...

If I could feel your love
I would have a better chance
Of believing.

We exchanged our vows long ago,
Vows of faith, love, and trust.
And from that day on
You apparently thought
It never needed to be said again.

But that's not the kind of man I am.

I live to feel the gentle touch,
The unsolicited one,
That now only comes
But once a week.

If I could feel your love

I might be stronger...

CANDELABRAS AND SCARLET TIGHTS

Have you ever had one of "those" nights? You know the kind, one that you hope no one ever remembers… Throughout my childhood, my family attended St. Paul United Methodist Church in Springfield, Missouri. One of the oldest congregations in town, it boasted several time-honored traditions in which various age groups participated. One such tradition, Ye Olde English Dinner, was one of the few in which the Youth Group played a key role. The youth of the church, which included the teens of junior high and high school, dressed up in Renaissance-era costumes, served a meal fit for a king, and entertained the crowd as well. The event, complete with lavish ceremonies and processions, included its own king and queen, chosen from the seniors in the Youth Group.

I never attended Ye Olde English Dinner as a child, although I recall my two older siblings being involved in it when they were old enough to be part of the Youth Group. As a youngster I always looked up to the kids in the Youth Group, as I thought they were the "cool" people, and longed for the day when I would be old enough to join their ranks.

Finally I entered seventh grade at the age of 12, and was officially welcomed into the Youth Group and all the mysteries of their secret order. Not only did they have their own regular Sunday School class, but on Sunday night, they got to meet in their "lounge" in the basement, which included couches, a pool table, air hockey game, and a stereo. Ooooh, I finally became one of the cool people!

That December, before I turned 13, Ye Old English Dinner was scheduled, and I was finally going to be part of it. Never having been to the event, I had no idea what to expect, but was ready to slip into a role and talk with the best fake English accent I could muster.

Before I go any further, allow me to say that if a court jester would have been one of the roles available, I would have grabbed it in a heartbeat. I considered myself funny enough to fill such a role. I don't know if anyone agreed, but I certainly wanted to give it a try. But alas, no such role existed. I had to take whatever part the organizers offered, and for us younger folks, the choices were minimal. I found myself assigned to serve as a Torchbearer.

Not knowing the first thing about medieval banquets, other than what I had gleaned from history class or saw on television, I had no idea what I was supposed to do as a Torchbearer. However it sounded like fire was involved so I was on board. Deep down inside I hoped for something impressive, lots of flames and danger, and that I would get to wear armor or something else really masculine.

With no advance rehearsals for the event, I had to wait until that night to get my costume and find out what my job entailed. All of us had to get dressed, run through the plan for the event one time, then do it for real with guests present. That was it. So that night when the time arrived to pass out costumes, I pushed and shoved my way to the front of the line, so that I could get my armor, deer hides, or whatever other studly gear as quickly as possible. I planned then to spend the rest of the night strutting around in all my pubescent manliness, attracting the throngs of big-eyed giggly junior high girls in Youth Group. All four of them.

The first thing they handed me was nylon tights. Scarlet nylon tights. And scarlet slippers.

My heart sunk. No armor, no deer hides. Instead, scarlet tights and slippers. Plus big poofy shorts and a velvet jacket, and to top it all off, a round velvet hat with feathers. My only chance left for a manly presence was the hope that I would carry something with flames leaping about.

After changing into my costume and discovering to my horror that the scarlet tights fit so snug that I had to switch from bass to tenor, I walked carefully out of the basement bathroom and into the dining hall, where the props, and hopefully my leaping flames, awaited.

I found Max, the father of one of the Youth Group's cool high schoolers, handling the props. He took one look at me and said, "Ah, a torchbearer. Here you go, son. We will light that just before you go out for the real thing."

He handed me a large wrought iron candelabra which to my 12-year-old arms weighed about 125 pounds. Struggling to tame the iron beast, I looked up to see what flaming madness he planned to light, imagining cauldrons filled with diesel fuel. There, in an upside-down V arrangement, were three small white candles. No cauldrons. No diesel fuel. No large flames in my future. I resolved myself to the fact that the night was not made for love nor hormones, and I hoped that no photographs of the evening would ever find their way to the general population of Harry P. Study Junior High.

I wrestled my iron crappy-candle gorilla to the hallway and sat down on an old pew to collect whatever shred of self-respect I had left. I realized that no matter how small the candles or constricting the tights, I had to put on the best show possible, and let the masses marvel at my torchbearer-ness.

Time passed slowly in the quiet, lonely basement, then finally the time came to do a quick run-through. My friend Mark served as fellow torchbearer, and we both complimented each other on the ridiculousness of our apparel. Moving into the dining hall wrestling our candelabras, we learned that our only duty was to walk through the dining hall ahead of the main procession of lords and ladies, and then each of us had to walk down the center aisles between long tables where the guests were to be seated, then leave the dining hall. It seemed simple enough, and we executed our jobs perfectly during the rehearsal. We were ready.

Within about half an hour, people began to file down the stairs and take their places in the dining hall. Watching as they made their way in, I recognized one lady as my mother's hairdresser, Nancy. (I secretly had a crush on her, but then again at that age I had a crush on any female that smelled nice.) I assumed she was there at the beckoning of my mother and was happy to see a friendly face. She waved then filed into the room with the rest of the people.

At 7:00 sharp, Max the prop dad called Mark and I over and lit our crappy little candles. Making sure to hold them at the proper height to prevent setting the drop ceiling on fire, we waited for the trumpeters to spit their announcement that the procession was on its way. Sounding more like kazoos than trumpets, the announcement was made, and Mark and I walked in at the head of the procession.

Looking as serious as possible, we walked into the dining hall, knowing all eyes were on us as we brought forth great light from our crappy candles. We rounded the corner at the end of the tables, and at the precisely correct moment, Mark and I broke off from each other and proceeded down the aisle between the guests seated at the long rows of tables.

One thing for which I did not prepare myself was how much more narrow my passage would become once guests were seated. What was once a sprawling aisle now had been whittled down to a space about two feet wide through which to carry my 125-pound iron beast with its crappy candles. Forward I went through the hungry masses.

As I walked, I became aware of an occasional mysterious vibration in my candelabra. I felt a somewhat intense pulse, followed by smaller reverberations. Not sure what to think of the phenomenon, I pressed on, still feeling the vibrations.

Then, when I was about one-fourth of the way down the aisle, I felt another vibration, followed by an audible "Ouch!" emanating from a male voice. Being a studious 12-year-old, I quickly discovered the source of the mysterious vibrations and voice of protest: I had been carrying the candelabra too low, and successfully beaned about twelve tall men seated on either side of the aisle. The pulse was felt each time I whacked one of them in the side of their head.

Rather than subject myself to the embarrassment of hearing both tables yell "Duck!" as I walked by, I quickly decided to raise up the candelabra another foot, thus clearing the tallest heads along both tables.

Satisfied with my handling of the situation, I pressed forward majestically in all my embarrassing regalia.

About halfway down the aisle, I passed Nancy, my mother's hairdresser. Conveniently seated on my side, I was glad she was short and the candelabra was higher, so that no negative report of bruising would reach my mother at her next appointment. As I passed Nancy, she leaned back and said quietly, "Nice legs". She had a sharp wit, and I knew she was messing with me. But being a goofy 12-year-old, I didn't have an immediate comeback. But about five seconds later, when I was eight or ten people past her, a notion of comedic genius struck me.

When I said earlier that I was a studious 12-year-old, it did not mean that I had anything resembling a mature sense of humor. Nor a filter. Nor was I a comedic genius.

So from a distance of about ten feet or so, I decided to yell back at her, "I SHAVED THEM JUST FOR YOU!"

And then I hit someone else in the head.

Noticing several heads turning to see who yelled about shaving something, and then one man looking to see who hit him in the head, I decided to make my exit. My majestic time on the floor with my iron beast and crappy candles completed, I beat a hasty retreat to the door of the dining hall. I'm not sure who got to the bathroom first to change, me or Mark. Within seconds, I was back in my hand-me-down jeans and flannel shirt, happy to be rid of the constricting scarlet tights so that my voice could return to its normal temblor.

I ate dinner alone in the church kitchen, hoping that no one would see me and recognize me as the head-bruiser guy who shaved something.

The rest of the dinner progressed well without my assistance, and I found myself happy to sit quietly in the back seat on the drive home. My older siblings apparently were not informed of my performance that evening, and word never got back to me that Nancy told Mom of my loud and poorly timed shaving announcement.

During my next five years of involvement in the Youth Group, I made sure I had other commitments on the night of Ye Old English Dinner. But I would have considered showing up if word got out that diesel fuel and looser tights would finally be involved...

CHRISTMAS PAST AND PRESENT

I find fond memories of Christmas past
In the twinkle of my toddler son's eyes
As he looks upon his Christmas tree
And points at all the lights.

I remember magic nights when I was young
Lying beneath the glowing tree,
Looking up through the lighted branches,
Gazing at the menagerie.

I remember long ago
The lights of the downtown square.
Peering through windows at mechanized toys,
Studying all that was there:

A bouncing Santa playing piano,
Little boys and girls in a row
Tapping feet, clapping hands,
Elves with gifts in tow.

I heard carols throughout the department store,
Saw wreaths, tinsel, and lights.
Santa was taking orders in the basement.
An atmosphere sure to excite.

Last night my son met Santa for the first time,
Perched warily upon his knee.
Not quite sure of what to think of the big man in red,
He kept looking back at me.

I look forward to future Christmas seasons,
Creating special memories for my little boy.
May he someday have a child of his own
And share his memories of Christmas joy.

JOSEPH'S PRAYER

Oh to the Heavens I lift my eyes, heavy laden with tears.
I am so filled this lonely night with a multitude of fears.
I look to this woman, riding the slow borrowed beast.
Her burden of child will be coming soon,
But Mary does not fear in the least.

But I fear.
Oh, worried am I.
This woman to me is so new.
We come together, she carries a child,
Belonging not to me, but to whom?

She says this child was not conceived of an earthly man.
She says she's been blessed by God above,
And for this child, He has a plan.

Tell me then, am I to become the father of God's Son on Earth?
My hands are not smooth but callused,
Bearing scars of my labor and thirst.
I am a man, just a man, a builder, carpenter by trade.
How can I be the chosen man to care for the mother and babe?

Dear God,
Grant me peace this night as I struggle with the task ahead.
Grant that we may in Bethlehem's gates find comfort
In a warm bed.

And grant your blessings, I pray, dear God,
On this beautiful woman and birth.
May she bring forth a wondrous child,
And may You be glorified here on Earth.

And thank you, for allowing me to be part of it.

Amen.

CHICAGO FOG

A heavy fog enshrouds the city,
Separating man from his steel shrines.
Reduced eyesight dims the world beyond
And the city transforms to a Monetian haze.

The metal rattle from El above and Metro nearby
Quiets as all becomes dampened, dimmed.
The roar of life becomes but a whisper
As in snow.

Have you ever had a kidney stone? To say they are painful is an understatement. Personally, I have given birth to nearly 20, much to my dismay. If you haven't had one, be happy and keep drinking lots of water. If you have given birth to one or more of these little stones, read on and see if you agree. And keep drinking lots of water...

KIDNEY STONE #3

I wake from sleep,
Ill from the pain
Which has interrupted
My friend Slumber.

The wound burns like fire
In the depth of my side
As I reach for help
Though none is there.

I writhe for two hours,
Hallucinating from pain.
Prayers for relief
Turn to quiet sobs.

Sedated to calm
The pain drives on
As a cool cloth
Soothes my brow.

My pain subsides

In a sudden flash
And I work my way back
To my friend Slumber.

And I pray the pain
Is gone to stay—
As sedation takes over—
I think I'll be okay—

LOVE AND CANDY

"Is love part candy?"
My child inquired of me;
Little did he understand the depth
Of the question posed innocently.

Is love part candy?
Should it be so sugary sweet?
Is love part candy
Or must it be something more deep?

I know of love as candy
in a relationship's early time.
Sticky sweet kisses, special touches,
Loving looks from eyes that shine.

Yet some base their love on that candy
And feel it must always be there,
Lest their love fade away
And they leave each other bare.

Others base their relationship
On raw physical desire.
Yet that type of thing may not last long
And it soon loses its fire.

Yet there are those lucky pairs
Who mix friendship, faith and trust
Together with love's candy,
For all those ingredients are a must.

Truly love must have a solid core
Upon which to build a life,
As vows exchanged express permanency
When two become husband and wife.

Yes, my son, love is part candy
And may you someday grow to learn
Of the many other sides of true love
When for someone's heart you'll yearn.

In the mid to late 1990s, I struggled with several personal issues, and found solace in much of Melissa Etheridge's music. Her powerful, soulful lyrics spoke to me, and I spent many nights carried away by her melodies back up by a solid band. Then one night I got to see her live in concert, seated just a few feet from the stage. A magical experience of sight and sound, I thought about it for several days, and came up with this, dedicated to her and the part her music played in getting me through those rough times.

Soul Mate

Woman, in my ears,
In my head,
In my soul...

You sing the songs
Which keep me company
Through my lonely nights
And troubled times.

The power of your messages
Pushes me,
And makes me long to be
More than I am.

You sing of hunger,
Pain within,
And the agony of love lost.

We share similar pain,
You and I,
Though our lives are so different,
With different catalysts.

Yet you are my Soul Mate,
As you continue to lift me up,
Make me think on a higher plane,
And breathe life into my creativity.

You have a brother.
You've just never met him.

My wife Lisa and I travelled more than usual in 2019. She served as the president of ACTFL, the national organization for language teachers. As President she had to attend and often speak at numerous conferences across the country. I felt fortunate to accompany her on most of those trips, getting to play tourist while she worked at the conferences.

One particularly lucky gig was Myrtle Beach, South Carolina. I had never before been there, so Lisa told me I needed to make sure I spent some time enjoying the beach. So I took her up on the offer. I rented a little cabana shelter, dug my feet into the sand, and spent the day listening to the ocean and getting sunburned. I also took my trusty writing journal with me, and penned the following:

THE BEACH

I've stood upon mountaintops
And listened to the silence.

I've laid in the midst of the forest
And sung with the trees.

But today I lie in the sand
With my face to the sun
And let the ocean
Make love to my soul.

SUCCESS

How is a man judged a success?
Is it by the number of digits in his paycheck?
Or the number of titles after his name?
Or how many times he beat somebody
With a better idea?

And who is the judge?
The person who signs the check?
The colleague at the coffee pot?
The secretary?

Success is a loving wife who's always there.
Success is always being there for the loving wife.
Success is a little child who squeals "Daddy!"
Success is squealing for the little child.
Success is making the boss happy.
Success is being happy with the boss.
Success is home.
Success is health.
Success is living.

And I'll be the judge...

The Eleventh Hour

Today is the day
I knew surely would come
When I had to pay
For the things I have done.

They've brought us out,
My companion and I.
We've been put on trial
And sentenced to die.

I've climbed a great hill
Under watchful eye
From soldiers below
And above, a big sky.

Soldiers stand around,
One on bent knee.
I hear much screaming
And realize it's me.

I feel quite ill
As the spikes drive deep.
I wish all could be reversed
And I could wake from sleep.

We are not alone
On this mount of sand
For between my friend and I
Is another man.

He wears on his head
A ring of thorns.
Some are calling it a crown
Amidst their other scorns.

He has endured great pain
And been much quieter than I.
He is so still
Yet is about to die.

Soldiers and some people there
Continue to chide
While others stand quietly,
Tears they try to hide.

I know of this man.
I have heard of his name.
They call him Teacher, Master—
Yet he has come under blame.

This man just said, "Father,"
And looked up to the sky.
Whose son is he
But God most high?

The crowd continues
To chide and harass;
My companion has joined them.
I must speak alas!

"Do you not fear God,"
I ask my friend,
"Since you are under
The same sentence condemned?"

"We indeed justly,
Due reward for our deeds.
This man has not wronged!"
My weary breast heaves.

I say to the man, "Jesus,"
In this late hour,
"Remember me
When you come in your kingly power."

He turns and looks at me
With soft loving eyes.
"Truly, I say to you today
You will join me in Paradise."

I rest my head back now
As my body grows weak.
I fear not death,
Forgiveness did I seek.

The day grows dark

And I am ready.

STAGE BLOOD AND FRENCH FRIES

In the spring of 2012, my son Corey and I stumbled upon an extraordinary opportunity: we were given the chance to be extras in a movie.

As a Civil War reenactor, I had received many requests through the years to show up in uniform at area events to visit with people and provide a presence harkening back to the 1800s. Corey joined me in reenacting in 2009, and we enjoyed participating in the hobby together. Then that spring in 2012, we learned that a production company was beginning to film scenes for an historical movie being shot in Taney County. The movie was about the Baldknobbers, a group of vigilantes that wreaked havoc in a few lawless counties in post-Civil War Missouri. Many of the scenes in the movie were to be filmed on the sites where the actual events took place. So it sounded like a very special project, and we were excited to be invited to participate. We learned that the opening scene of the movie was to be a flashback to the aftermath of a battle. As Civil War reenactors we were to play dead soldiers on the field for this scene.

When we arrived at the site, Corey and I found several other reenactor friends present, all of us thrilled to have the chance to be in the movie. It took quite a while to get everything situated as the director and camera operator walked over the field and planned the shoot.

Finally the director, Michael Johnson, came over to our cluster of reenactors.

"Who is the highest ranking officer here?" Michael inquired.

Several of us looked at each other, and it became obvious that as a captain, I was the ranking officer. So without knowing what lay in store, I raised my hand and said, "Apparently I am!"

"Ok, come with me," Michael grinned, grabbing me by the arm.

We walked across the field to a level spot selected by Michael and the cameraman.

"I'm going to have you lay right here," Michael directed, and filled me in on what I was to do, which essentially was lay there and, well, play dead. "Before you get settled in, go over there and let our makeup lady get you squared away. We need you guys to be a bit messy."

I drove my sword into the ground to mark the spot where I was supposed to lay, then walked back across the field to Brooke for makeup. Meanwhile Michael gave direction to the rest of the guys, telling them where and how he wanted them to lay. My buddy Scott ended up sprawling over the trunk of a fallen tree, while his son Zach took a position laying over some large branches. Corey, placed in a hollowed out spot under the same tree, had the shadiest spot of the whole group.

Brooke, busily applying a nasty prosthetic belly wound on another actor when I got to her area, asked me to stand at the nearby trucks until she was ready for me. As I waited, the rest of my reenactor buddies came over, as they needed the same makeup treatment that I was awaiting.

Finally she was done with the actor, and turned to us to ask who wanted to be first. I stepped forward, figuring the sooner I got made up the sooner I could get back to my spot on the field. She recruited another lady on the crew to help work on us so that they could get each of us made up twice as fast. They put dirt and mud on our faces and uniforms, then squirted stage blood in and down the sides of our mouths, and dripped it out of our ears. They even packed gritty soil under our fingernails.

After all that, Corey and I walked back to the filming area to grab a little shade before taking our places. We chuckled as we looked each other over, shaking our heads.

"We look like thirty different kinds of hell," Corey

laughed.

The rest of the reenactors eventually made their way over, and we visited and laughed till it was time to get ready to make some movie magic. We took our places again, and I laid down as previously directed, noticing that there was no shade to be found in that spot. Michael came over to adjust how he wanted me to lie on the ground, as he wanted me posed in a certain position. In the scene, another actor was to walk up to my spot, lean over and drink from my canteen, steal my pistol, then walk to the fallen tree where the other dead soldiers lay strewn. After a couple of adjustments, my position on the ground met with their satisfaction, and everyone was ready to start filming. I closed my eyes but not before checking to see if any vultures were circling overhead. You never know.

As expected, it took several hours to shoot the entire scene. Fortunately we took a break about two hours into filming, and the crew brought out water bottles for everyone. We appreciated the water, as we hadn't eaten nor drank anything since arriving at the site. It also felt good to sit up for a while and open my eyes, as I had to keep them closed throughout the filming.

After the brief respite, it was time to get back to filming, so I settled in once again on the hard ground in my somber death pose and closed my eyes. Filming went on for another two hours, then finally Michael called it a wrap. We gathered for a cast and crew photo, and then were dismissed to go home.

As Corey and I walked to my truck, we took inventory of our appearance. A bit swollen and sunburned from roasting in that open field, I ached from the time spent on the ground. Looking at each other, we both had all the dirt, mud and stage blood still on us. We certainly looked like we lost whatever fight we were in. And we were starving. So without cleaning up or changing out of our Civil War uniforms, we headed out for the 30-mile trip back to Springfield.

When we reached town, we decided to head for the drive-thru at McDonalds to eat then continue driving. It was only after I ordered that I realized we still looked really bad and bloody. But there wasn't anything we could do about it, so forward we went. I pulled up to the pay window with a big bloody smile on my face like absolutely nothing was wrong. The girl at the window did a double-take, eyes wide as saucers, and took my money. As we pulled forward to the pick-up window, she must have yelled something to the rest of the crew. The lady there looked scared to death, quickly gave me our drinks then asked me to pull up into the drive-thru parking space to wait for our food. I just smiled another big bloody grin and pulled into the slot to wait.

Finally, after a few minutes, the manager came out with our burgers. He handed the bag of food to me, skeptically looked us over with a troubled half-smile and said "Here you go. You boys be careful!"

We just gave another bloody smile and said, "Will do!"

It felt good to finally eat, and we had a good laugh about the looks we got from the McDonald's crew. We sat there in the cab of my truck, wolfing down our burgers and fries, guessing they had quite the conversation about us and how bad we looked. Corey then turned and looked out the window.

"Hey there's a Walmart over there! I need some –"

There was a pause and he turned and we looked at each other, then looked down at ourselves and our condition. We gave each other a bloody smile.

"I'll wait," he said.

A Soldier's Tale

My sweet precious wife, do not cry
As the sounds of war grow near.
I take my place in the rank and file
And ask you not to fear.

Your delicate perfumed kerchief
I lovingly pin to my weathered shell.
It is the perfect reminder, my dear,
Of your delicate form I remember well.

I'll fight for you bravely, swear do I.
Defending you and our home, I will give all.
My name will be remembered for my deeds
Should I be struck and fall.

If this is truly to be
My last day on this beloved earth,
Please bury my body under the old oak tree,
The one planted well before my birth.

And my beloved, please tell our sons
Of the bravery their father displayed.
Teach them to be men of integrity,
To live their lives in an honorable way.

Do not cry, my sweet love,
As the acrid smoke fills the air.
I will return if Providence allows,
Return to your tender care.

Home seems so very far away now
As we encounter our foe yet again.
Your favor still clings to my bloodied coat
As I continue on through the din.

The smoke is so thick it stings the eyes
And robs the straining warrior of his breath.
The heat, it stifles. The noise, it deafens.
And behind me, beside me, in front of me is death.

Oh God, what is this pain here in my chest
And why am I on the ground?
I was standing over there getting ready to fire.
Why in the world am I down?

I look down to where your favor has been pinned,
Reminding me of your love.
The delicate kerchief is nowhere to be found,
Replaced by a large hole and my blood.

There's your kerchief, I see it now,
I now hold it in my hand.
Damn, this wound hurts so very bad.
I long for my homeland.

Bandaged up, now here I lay,
My mind filled with thoughts of you.
The wound leaves me quite short of breath
But my life is not yet through.

I now walk many miles each day,
As my fighting time is now done.
Crossing over just one more hill,
Our home bids a fond welcome.

Oh dear lord, I see you!
You're running out to greet me home!
I see our boys come running too!
My, my, how much they have grown!

Oh my God, the pain again!
Why do I feel it so?
I open my eyes, and I'm still on the field,
Nowhere did I go.

I feel so weak, the pain is so great,
I can barely sit up to see
My brothers in arms strewn all about,
Lost the battle did we.

I must lie back again now,
Your favor still in my hand.
A great light appears before me,
And -

THE SHOEBOX HAT STORY

Sometimes creativity goes incredibly unappreciated...
    I started kindergarten in the fall of 1970 at Westport Elementary, excited to finally be a student at the same school as my big brother and sister. Back then, kindergarten classes were only half-day, and I was enrolled in the afternoon class. Several kids from that same class are still my dearest friends, and we stay in contact quite regularly. Two buddies of mine, Greg and Ross, have unfortunately been lost to time, as I do not recall their last names and they moved away at some point. I still have a picture of Greg from kindergarten or first grade, but not of Ross. However there is one event that took place with Greg and Ross that stands out in my memory.

At some point in the spring of that school year, Greg, Ross and I decided we were going to have a car club during recess. We planned to bring our toy cars (Hot Wheels or Matchbox) and at recess we were going to play with them near a small drainage ditch in the playground. A drainpipe daylighted there, and the erosion around it made a great path for running toy cars along the washed-out areas and through the patches of grass around it.

So the next morning, I collected a bunch of my cars from my vast collection and put them in a little green cardboard shoe box to safeguard them until recess. Unfortunately in my packing fury, I forgot one of the important car club rules: you had to wear a hat to play. My favorite hat, red with a baseball patch on it that said "Little Slugger", was left behind.

When I got to school, we three boys huddled together in a corner, looking at each other's cars, comparing the paint jobs and whether or not they had doors that opened. Excited to have our first car club at recess, we kept looking at each other as the time neared. Finally, recess came and we grabbed our boxes of cars and ran outside to the drainage ditch.

Arriving at the drainpipe, we dumped out our cars in little piles. Ross and Greg put on their hats and I started running my cars around the eroded areas near the pipe. I noticed Greg and Ross weren't playing yet, so I looked up and they were staring at me.

"Where's your hat, Timmy?" Ross asked me.

"I forgot it," I admitted, mortified.

"You gots to wear a hat for the car club!" Ross scolded.

Looking around, I grabbed my little green cardboard shoe box and put it on my head. It fit perfectly on the sides and did a rather nice job of keeping the sun out of my eyes. I smiled, impressed with my own ingenuity, plus I thought I looked fairly dashing with a green cardboard shoe box on my head.

Greg and Ross kept staring at me, now scowling.

I just pointed at the box and said, "This is my hat. Let's play."

I spent the entire recess playing with my shoe box on my head, proud of such an innovative hat idea.

We never had the car club again at recess. And obviously using a cardboard shoe box as a hat never caught on as an acceptable fashion statement.

A Long Farewell

I knew this moment would come soon,
But that doesn't make it any easier.
I've provided for you the best I could
And tried to make your life
Up to now
Happy.

Yet you feel the need to go;
Though you have never actually said it,
I could tell you were needing something,
That extra something,
To make your life
Happy.

I can't help the pain I feel right now.
I hope you don't think it foolish;
I just have a hard time letting go
Of our life together
Which was
Happy.

So we must now make our silent farewell,
For in this silence there is dignity
And with our dignity, pride
So that we each
May leave
Happy.

So go ahead and swim away.
The cats were going to kill you anyway.

TUMMY TROUBLE BLUES
(a bit of silliness)

Sitting at home on Sunday night,
My tummy at once began gurgling.
I began to ponder what caused such,
Was it the Sick Bug come burgling?

As day ended, on came night,
And the gurglings grew more odd
I soon realized my hideous fate -
I was to pray to the porcelain god.

Like a gazelle (a heavily sedated gazelle)
I trudged up the dark stairs.
The pain in my gut was much like that
Of pulling nose hairs.

So the bathroom exhaust fan quickly became
My closest worldly friend.
After giving back my previous dinner,
I wanted it all to end.

Ah, the cool washcloth I did savor,
A gift from my loving wife.
She threw it at me from a great distance,
Obviously fearing for her life.

Finally I made it to the bed,
Horizontal life felt good to me
And I hoped sleep would soon come
And allow me a reprieve.

Ah, sleep...

My Boot Passion

So I have this passion, this thing about fashion,
This thing for what you wear.
So I get all excited, I get so delighted
By the things you put here and put there.

And the constant craving, the wild mindless raving
Of seeing you before me in soft leather boots.
Oh, the things in my mind (they're there all the time);
Your leather-clad legs in my hands.

This desire is so strong, it's been there all along,
To see boots over a bare leg or hose.
I'm certain it comes from an early childhood crush
On Nancy Sinatra's album cover pose.

So, my yummy wife, love of my life
You're about to see my passion shift from low to high;
Slip those boots on for me, and please let me see
As the zipper climbs up your delicious thigh.

Wearing boots is so sexy; I find it perplexy
Why others don't feel as I do.
So keep wearing the boots if you it well suits
And watch me go crazy over you.

This is yet another example of a Frantic Poem. While its subject matter lacks the gloominess of "I Quit" (page 51), it still requires the reader to refrain from taking a breath until coming to a period. Rather than addressing a sad or frightening situation, this fun and lighthearted Frantic Poem deals with someone trying desperately to express feelings of love and desire but gets a little carried away, and thus becomes frantic. Enjoy.

Don't Forget to Breathe

Next to you in a public room
As some people's world goes by with a zoom
My heart pounds with an audible boom
And I find myself glad that you're mine.

I've tried and I've tried to remain from obsession
But dammit I want you as my own possession
And my previous times have taught me a lesson
And that lesson is truly you are the one
Who can make my life a burden or pleasure
And I know I have love's true treasure
And I can't live without you by any measure—
I'm ranting and raving now, aren't I?

You are my one love, I cannot deny,
My feelings for you are so strong inside,
And I'm afraid I cannot equally hide
The fact that you turn me on.

I look at you and your pretty hair,
I study the sight of you standing there
And I become increasingly aware
That you take my breath away.

So forgive me if I seem just a bit looney
And ramble on like a horrid Andy Rooney--
You know, I can't think of anything else that ends with "ooney"
So I'll just close—

I love you, by the way.

AMIDST THE SQUIRM

A dark blue room
Moves in a singular squirm
As the walls reverberate
The explosive roar.

My heart pounds
As I stand alone,
Scanning the room,
Seeing nothing and everything.

An errant strobe
Illuminates a second's experience.
In that moment's flash
I capture your image.

Black hair, black glasses, black dress,
Black heels.
I feel you see me
Before you disappear.

High over the squirm
I look for your image
Yet the next errant strobe
Reveals emptiness where you were.

I search to find you
And amidst the movement
A body stands still
Looking at me, into me.

I push through the squirm
To the island you are.
Cradling your face
I taste your mystery.

Our lips part.
I remove your glasses,
Take your hand
And surround you with me
As we join the squirm.

We dance without words
As a bead of sweat
Trickles down my temple.
I hold you closer.

Woman in black,
In my arms,
We move as one
Amidst the squirm.

LAY DOWN

Lay down now, remove the thoughts
That cloud your busy mind.
Close your eyes, and let your hands fall open.

Breathe slowly, as I loosen your belt
And let go, as your shoes come off.

There is no need to fear anymore;
You should know better.
I'll not hurt you, nor take away your soul.

I love you more than you could ever know
And I want to show you....

A gentle kiss I will place atop your foot,
A soft caress upon your knee,
The glide of my tongue along your waist.

My fingers will dance around your every curve
And my soul will be yours

As it was when we first kissed.

WEARING THE BOOTS

Would you wear your boots
If I ask you to?

Would you let me touch you
If I ask nicely?

Could I just stare at you
As you lie there next to me?

If you wear the boots,
Yes, it will be intense.
I will caress you
With my tongue,
From the luscious boots
To your soft ears.

I will shake all over
From the charge of the moment
And will caress you
And stare...

If you let me touch you,
It will be gentle
And loving
And soft

And I hope you will close your eyes

And lay back
And enjoy
As my fingers tour your lovely self.

But it's not just about
Wearing boots.
It's also a question - -

Do you love me enough
To do something special
Just for me?

Will you wear your boots?

PASSION

Dancing around each other
By the light of the full moon--
I see your smooth skin
And smell your perfume.

We stand five feet from each other
Though if we were pressed together
It would not be close enough.

Come here.

Allow me to hold you closely,
My hand gently resting in the small of your back.
Come so close I can feel your breath
And hear you think.

I long to taste your delicate lips
And savor the drops from your tongue.
Scrape your fingernails across my cheek
And feel me against you.

I remain your obsessed lover,
Ready at any moment
To draw you to me
And make love to you.

THE RIDE

Take each other by the hand
And hold on tight--
The brake has been released.

Try not to fear the unknown on this ride
As it has been that way
Since you were born.

Don't mistake the fear
As a wedge keeping you apart.
It is also the delicate string
Which holds you together.

You'll survive and even enjoy the ride
As long as you ride together.
It's normal to be afraid at times,
Just be sure to go through it together.

We are all at different places along this ride,
And we are here to help.

Just remember:

Always ride together

And talk each other through

And together you'll enjoy the ride.

A Dance with Jami

Back in my college days, Dad had his own country music band, and played Friday and Saturday nights at a place called the Boondocks Saloon and Dance Hall. Situated in an old refurbished barn on an outer road that ran along Interstate 44 near Chesapeake, MO, it served as the home bar for Dad's band for a few years. I was only about 20, and my sister Kathy was a tender 15, but the owners of the bar, Larry and Sylvia, had no problem with us being there, since we sat with Mom the whole night, and they knew we had no intention of causing trouble. We sat at the "Band Table" and drank Cokes all night while listening to the music. Occasionally Kathy and I got up and danced around the floor together, figuring out something similar to a modified two-step.

Being a young man with active hormones, I often scanned the room just in case some single young lady showed up in need of attention. Typically no such woman ever appeared. The folks usually in attendance were at least in their 30s, and often there were a few folks in their 60s and 70s. Most couples got up from time to time to enjoy the dance floor together.

The Boondocks had a big square wooden dance floor, situated in front of the bandstand, running half the length of the old barn, easily accommodating 50 dancing couples at once. At the beginning of each night, before many people showed up, either Larry or Sylvia walked along the dance floor and sprinkled corn meal on the floor to make it more slippery for folks who wanted to slide their boots as they danced.

Sitting there eyeballing the room one night, I zeroed in on a young blonde waiting tables in the room. Straining to see through the dimly lit barn, she looked to be barely 21.

Determined to find out more, I decided to approach Sylvia and simply asked who she was. She told me the girl's name was Jami, and with a wink added that she was single.

"I'll remember that," I told Sylvia, returned the wink and thanked her as I walked off.

Later that night, Jami and I nearly collided as she was dashing around to take care of the many patrons filling the tables around the dance floor. I introduced myself, which gave me the opportunity to shake her very soft hand. We chatted briefly, then parted so that she could get back to work. Occasionally she came over to check on our table to see if we needed anything. Each time she walked away, I turned and looked at Mom, raising my eyebrows.

One night, as I sat there listening to the band, Jami suddenly appeared out of the shadows and grabbed my arm, pulling me to the dance floor as a slow song started.

"Come on, I've got a few minutes. Let's dance!" she hollered over the music.

I smiled, realizing she could have grabbed any man in the room, but she chose me. She wanted to dance with *me*.

Getting over my shock, I slipped my right arm around the small of her back as she held onto my arm. I drew her in close, pulling her right hand into my chest, and she snuggled in to me as we moved across the floor, resting the side of her face against mine. My face was buried in her wispy blonde hair, intoxicating me with the smell of her powdery perfume. It was an oasis of sweet aroma in a room full of stale cigarette smoke.

We spoke not a word, moving as a solitary silhouette across the floor, her boots and my shoes barely touching the floor. I could feel her heart beating, making me wish the song would play forever. I held her so close I could feel every button on her western shirt. Her breath on my neck was like a warm wet breeze, and I wanted to taste her lips.

I turned her slowly left, then right, then left again as we moved around the floor. I wondered if her eyes were closed.

The song drew to a close, and I pulled her to me briefly, as she wrapped her arms around my neck.

"Thank you," she said, as softly as you can in a crowded bar.

"You're welcome, and thank you," I said in her ear, and kissed her cheek.

Our bodies parted, but we still held on, our hands sliding down each other's arm. The last pieces of us to let go were our fingertips.

Jami went back to waiting tables, and I walked slowly across the bar, back to my table, with a smile on my face. Sitting down, I was greeted with stares from everyone seated there, all with "what the hell was that" looks on their faces.

I just sat back and smiled, hoping for another slow song.

MISSING YOU

It catches up with me
In the dark of night;
That's when I feel most alone.

The fact that you're not here,
Lying next to me,
Is a Lonely that has no name.

I know it won't be too long
Before you're back in my arms,
And that's good to know.

But here in this moment,
In this darkness,
It feels like years.

I long for your touch
And the taste of your kiss
And to feel your breath upon my skin.

I tremble inside,
Whisper your name,
And count the seconds…

SUNDAY MORNING

Lost in this moment
Of the still dawning day,
Your hand on my shoulder,
Together we lay—

The room, barely light
As the outside world stirs;
The clock strikes six,
Two nearby cats purr.

You rise for a moment
To attend to your friends
But return again soon
To crawl under the covers again.

I roll over behind you,
Your hand cupped in mine,
And we drift back to sleep,
Our hearts intertwined.

DEVOTION

Tracing the contours of your face
With a slightly trembling finger,
I feel my heart soaring skyward,
Just like the first time I felt Love.

I burn to feel your lips on mine.
I crave the light scrape of your nails
As those long fingers caress my arms
And I am soothed to sleep.

I dance in the sparkle of your eyes.
In the softness of your skin I rest.
I breathe by the whisper of your voice
And I am nourished by your love.

I live through the day as your obsessed lover,
One who cannot get enough of you.
You are held in most high esteem
As my heart, soul and body are yours.

Yet I beg you do not take advantage
Of the power you have over me
For words of anger or rejection
Could draw blood and drain me of life.

I need your love to get through my days.
I crave your touch when alone.
I wish I could see your face before me now
So I could surround you and anchor me.

I want to breathe in the fragrance of your hair.
I want to walk up behind you quietly
And whisper my devotion ...

I love you.

MY LOVE, ASLEEP

I trace the outline
Of your soft sweet lips
With the tip of my finger.

I lean in close
As you sleep
To feel your breath upon my face.

Gently my arm circles you
To hold you close
In your faithful slumber

And amidst your sleep
You move forward
To curl up against me.

With silent pride
I kiss you,
My sleeping love.

PROCLAIMING MY LOVE

My heart swells
With so many wonderful feelings…

Thoughts of how much I love you,
Thoughts of how beautiful you are,
Thoughts of my great fortune
To be the man of your choosing.

To my eyes comes a mist
As I proclaim my love with this pen.
I want to cover you as a nourishing waterfall,
Letting my love flow over you
As I have seen water cover you
While together we bathed.

My love is to be a reassurance,
Your armor during dark days
When your tender, vulnerable side
Finds doubt or questions.

My love is to be your rock
When you need a firm foundation
Upon which to stand.

And my love is to share in your passion,
To fill you and cover you
With my adoration.

Come swim in my arms
And let me love you
Forever.

THE HEAVENS

I looked to the Heavens one evening
And wondered which star should be yours.
I pondered the sight, the majesty, the size
Of the lights shining amidst the darkness.

I looked first to the brightest star,
The one that shone above all others.
I noticed it to be a bit too bright,
Almost too showy,

And I knew it wasn't yours.

I looked to one of the dimmer stars,
The kind hardly seen without aid.
It seemed so hard to pick out,
So hidden by the others,

And I knew it wasn't yours.

I studied half a dozen more,
Trying hard to find the one
Yet the answer came,
As there it was all along..

There was not one single star for you,
No single star would do.

They are all yours.
They are all for you.

THOUGHTS OF SOMEONE

The feel of your sweater
The softness of your hair
The strength in your eyes
The warmth of your touch.

The awkward movements
Of our clumsy love
As glasses and noses collide
Just before we kiss.

Think about it...

You and I under a quilt
On a snowy night.
No lights on in the house
Except the Christmas tree.

You and I holding hands
On a sunny day
As we walk through the woods,
Pausing to kiss by the brook.

You and I holding each other
On a blanket by the fire,
Talking
And loving.

Heaven...

MORE...

Inject me with your soul.
Let me savor your spirit
As it rushes through my veins
Toward my heart.

My brain clouds quickly
With each throaty whisper.
Gazing into your soft eyes
I am mesmerized.

Long loving fingers caress my skin
As I taste your lips.
I am riding a wave
As I surrender to your power.

You are an addiction--
The prescription which saves me
From the grips of this life.
I am consumed by you.

VALENTINE'S DAY 2018

I thought I knew within my heart
How true love was supposed to be.
I thought I had it all figured out,
How it would feel between you and me.

But now I know, it's crystal clear
That back then I had no clue
Of the many pleasures awaiting me
And of the depth of love in you.

My heart now teems to overflowing,
A lump in my throat oft returns,
My eyes mist up, filled with emotion,
As flames of love within me steadily burn.

I thank you for choosing me, as I am,
And for your simple but life-changing "Hey You".
These months together have been filled with laughter,
Love and joy, such I never before knew.

Thank you also, my precious wife,
For the passion we have shared.
For the dancing, for the sweet soft kisses,
And for simply being there.

Thank you too, my beautiful Lisa,
For the frogs and kitty cats three,
For the pillows, books, and trips together.
We are indeed a pair, you and me.

I thank you finally, my sweet love,
For everything you are.
Thank you for loving me,
For your light that removes all dark.

I love you.

ABOUT THE AUTHOR

Photo by Erin Northrip
Gambles Photography

A native of Springfield, Missouri, Tim Ritter discovered writing and public speaking early in life. By age 13, he wrote two children's adventure books, several plays and created his own comic strip which eventually found its way to his junior high school newspaper. He also discovered that he liked being on stage, and how people tended to listen when he spoke into a microphone.

Throughout his professional career as a mechanical engineer, Tim wrote articles for trade magazines and was the featured speaker at hundreds of seminars across the country. However, his love of the written word compelled him to continue writing poetry and short stories throughout his adult life.

Now retired, Tim lives outside Fair Grove, Missouri, with his wife, Lisa, writing full time and speaking to civic groups and organizations on a variety of topics. He is a board member of the Springfield Writers Guild and a member of the Douglas County Historical Society, Ozarks Genealogical Society, and the Poe Studies Association.

OTHER BOOKS BY TIM RITTER

Sarah Burning is the true story of a tragic fatal housefire which occurred near Ava, Missouri in October of 1959. Beyond the story of that deadly night, however, is the courageous tale of the three survivors of the fire, and their struggle to put their lives back together and move forward.

The Lantern series of books is a collection of lectures which have been presented to Masonic lodges in Southwest Missouri and has received critical acclaim from Masons across the state.

Tim can be contacted via his website at timritter.net or by email at tritterman@gmail.com.

He can be found on Facebook at Author Tim Ritter, on Instagram at authortimritter, and Youtube at TimothyRitter.

www.ingramcontent.com/pod-product-compliance
Lightning Source LLC
Chambersburg PA
CBHW031445040426
42444CB00007B/975